# TEXT AND PERFORMANCE

*General Editor:* Michael Scott

The series is designed to introduce sixth-form and undergraduate students to the themes, continuing vitality and performance of major dramatic works. The attention given to production aspects is an element of special importance, responding to the invigoration given to literary study by the work of leading contemporary critics.

The prime aim is to present each play as a vital experience in the mind of the reader – achieved by analysis of the text in relation to its themes and theatricality. Emphasis is accordingly placed on the relevance of the work to the modern reader and the world of today. At the same time, traditional views are presented and appraised, forming the basis from which a creative response to the text can develop.

In each volume, Part One: *Text* discusses certain key themes or problems, the reader being encouraged to gain a stronger perception both of the inherent character of the work and also of variations in interpreting it. Part Two: *Performance* examines the ways in which these themes or problems have been handled in modern productions, and the approaches and techniques employed to enhance the play's accessibility to modern audiences.

A synopsis of the play is given and an outline of its major sources, and a concluding Reading List offers guidance to the student's independent study of the work.

D1555058

# TWELFTH NIGHT

## Text and Performance

### LOIS POTTER

MACMILLAN

First published 1985

Published by
Higher and Further Education Division
MACMILLAN PUBLISHERS LTD
Houndmills, Basingstoke, Hampshire RG21 2XS
and London
Companies and representatives
throughout the world

Typeset by
*Wessex Typesetters Ltd*
Frome, Somerset

Printed in Hong Kong

British Library Cataloguing in Publication Data
Potter, Lois
Twelfth night. – (Text and performance)
1. Shakespeare, William. Twelfth night
I. Title     II. Series
822.3'3     PR2837
ISBN 0–333–33995–9

# CONTENTS

Illustrations will be found in Part Two.

# ACKNOWLEDGEMENTS

All quotations from *Twelfth Night* are taken from the New Penguin Shakespeare edition (1968), edited by M.M. Mahood. Other Shakespeare quotations are from *The Complete Works* (1951), edited by Peter Alexander.

Source details for the illustrations are given with the relevant captions to the plates.

I should like to thank Robin Midgley, Julian Lopez-Morillas and Roger Warren for their help. I should also like to dedicate this book to Arthur Colby Sprague, who first taught me, and many others, the importance of considering plays as texts for performance.

# GENERAL EDITOR'S PREFACE

For many years a mutual suspicion existed between the theatre director and the literary critic of drama. Although in the first half of the century there were important exceptions, such was the rule. A radical change of attitude, however, has taken place over the last thirty years. Critics and directors now increasingly recognise the significance of each other's work and acknowledge their growing awareness of interdependence. Both interpret the same text, but do so according to their different situations and functions. Without the director, the designer and the actor, a play's existence is only partial. They revitalise the text with action, enabling the drama to live fully at each performance. The academic critic investigates the script to elucidate its textual problems, understand its conventions and discover how it operates. He may also propose his view of the work, expounding what he considers to be its significance.

Dramatic texts belong therefore to theatre and to literature. The aim of the 'Text and Performance' series is to achieve a fuller recognition of how both enhance our enjoyment of the play. Each volume follows the same basic pattern. Part One provides a critical introduction to the play under discussion, using the techniques and criteria of the literary critic in examining the manner in which the work operates through language, imagery and action. Part Two takes the enquiry further into the play's theatricality by focusing on selected productions of recent times so as to illustrate points of contrast and comparison in the interpretation of different directors and actors, and to demonstrate how the drama has worked on the modern stage. In this way the series seeks to provide a lively and informative introduction to major plays in their text and performance.

MICHAEL SCOTT

# PLOT SYNOPSIS AND SOURCES

Orsino, Duke of Illyria, is in love with the Countess Olivia, but she has vowed to spend seven years in seclusion, mourning her brother's recent death. Viola arrives on the coast of Illyria after a shipwreck in which she has lost her twin brother Sebastian. She disguises herself as a page named Cesario and takes service with the Duke. He sends her to Olivia's house. Unlike his other messengers, she succeeds in entering, but her efforts on Orsino's behalf result in Olivia's falling in love with the supposed page. Meanwhile, Viola herself has fallen in love with Orsino. Unknown to the other characters, Sebastian – in the company of Antonio, who saved him from drowning – has also come to Illyria.

Olivia's strict and humourless steward, Malvolio, has antagonised the rest of the household: her cousin Sir Toby Belch, the clown Feste, and her waiting woman Maria. In revenge, Maria forges a riddling love-letter to him, in Olivia's handwriting, inviting him to show that he returns her love by dressing and behaving in an absurd way. When he carries out these instructions, Olivia naturally thinks him a lunatic, which gives the conspirators an excuse for treating him like one.

Olivia's passion for Cesario has become obvious even to the foolish Sir Andrew Aguecheek, another of her suitors. Sir Toby eggs him on to challenge Cesario to a duel which neither of them wants. It is interrupted by Antonio, who thinks he is rescuing Sebastian again. When Antonio is arrested by Orsino's officers, Cesario denies all knowledge of him. The two knights pursue the page, but the person they meet is Sebastian, who gives as good as he gets. Olivia also meets Sebastian, and, for the first time, finds 'Cesario' responsive to her love.

Confusion is at its height – with Cesario accused of duplicity towards everyone – when Sebastian arrives and is reunited with his sister. Orsino recognises, and responds to, the love that Viola has shown him in her disguise; Olivia is happy to transfer her love to Sebastian. Malvolio learns of the trick that has been played on him and leaves, threatening revenge. Feste sings a farewell to the audience.

### SOURCES

The ultimate source for *Twelfth Night* is Plautus's *Menaechmi*, already used by Shakespeare for *The Comedy of Errors*. The play inspired many Renaissance adaptations, including *Gl'Ingannati* (discussed in Section 2), which was translated into French and thence into a Latin version performed at Cambridge in 1595. The story is also told in prose romances. Barnaby

Riche's *Farewell to Militarie Profession* (1581) includes the tale of 'Apolonius and Silla', adapted from a French version by Belleforest, which is itself based on an Italian original by Bandello. There is no known source for the Malvolio plot, though it is sometimes suggested that the feuds and rivalries of the Elizabethan court may have borne some relation to those in Olivia's household.

# PART ONE: TEXT

## 1  INTRODUCTION

Most of the early criticism of *Twelfth Night* is in fact theatrical criticism: that is, it comes from spectators rather than readers of the play. The first reference to it occurs in the diary of a young man, John Manningham, who was studying law at the Middle Temple, one of the London Inns of Court. He saw the play there, on 2 February 1602, at a special performance for the students and lawyers. It was Candlemas Day, the last day of their season of revels. He noted that the plot of the play reminded him of several earlier ones about twins: Plautus's *Menaechmi*, Shakespeare's own *Comedy of Errors*, and an Italian comedy called *Gl'Inganni* (*The Deceptions*). He went on to praise the 'good practice', or practical joke, which was played on Malvolio. This part of the story, presumably, was new to him.

The play seems to have been equally successful elsewhere. Verses published in 1640 declare that the public theatre was 'full To hear Malvolio, that cross-gartered gull'. We also know that the play was performed at Court in 1623 under the title *Malvolio*, and that Charles I, who owned a copy of the Shakespeare Folio, wrote this name opposite *Twelfth Night* in the list of contents. When the play was revived after the Civil War, another diarist, Samuel Pepys, recorded that he saw it three times, once on 6 January, Twelfth Night itself. But he found it 'silly' and 'not related at all to the name or day'.

This early evidence, skimpy as it is, suggests two conclusions. One is that the most memorable part of *Twelfth Night* was its intrigue, particularly the trick played on Malvolio. The other is that nobody really understood what the title meant, except perhaps that the play would be an appropriate choice for the holiday season. Much subsequent criticism has done little more than refine on, or disagree with, these two assumptions. *Is*

Malvolio the centre of the play? Does the title indicate that it is only a holiday romp, or does it hide some profound significance? What about the sub-title, *What You Will*? Is Shakespeare saying that he doesn't care what the play is called (or, for that matter, about anything else: note the repetition of 'that's all one' in the final scene and Feste's song)? Does he mean that he is writing for the audience's taste rather than his own, or that the play is about the effects of *will* (desire, or specifically sexual desire)? What about the fact that his name was Will – he had already punned on it in the sonnets – and that he was the father of twins, a boy and a girl?

My concern in this book will be only with questions which theatrical performance can attempt to answer. In the first part I shall consider some of the factors which make *Twelfth Night* such a complex piece of work: its thematic and literary context, the verbal and visual patterns which make up its structure. Then, because it seems to me a play whose theatrical history is often more illuminating than its criticism, I shall look at some of the interpretations reflected in productions of the past. This will form a prologue to the study of more recent productions which makes up Part Two.

## 2    INTERPRETING THE TITLE

The simplest way to look at *Twelfth Night* is in the context that Manningham's diary provides: one of several plays about twins and mistaken identity, where confusion rises to such a height that the characters wonder whether they, or others, have gone mad. The very names – *Errors, Deceptions* – are significant. They imply that the audience's pleasure will come from watching the characters make fools of themselves. In Plautus, as in Shakespeare's imitation, *The Comedy of Errors*, the confusion involves twins of the same sex, but in several Italian comedies, of which the earliest is *Gl'Ingannati* (*The Dupes*, 1538, by members of the Academy of the Intronati in Siena), the joke acquires another dimension when a girl dresses as a boy and is mistaken for her brother.

In the Latin and Italian comedies, the twin who becomes the object of the mistake takes advantage of it to exploit the other characters, both financially and sexually. *The Comedy of Errors* is different in that the heroes, though they are accused of such exploitation, are in fact innocent. In *Twelfth Night*, too, neither Viola nor Sebastian knowingly takes advantage of anyone. But a great deal of deception does go on in the play. Sir Toby gets money, and even a horse, out of Sir Andrew by flattering his hopes of winning the rich heiress Olivia. Maria gets a husband (Sir Toby) by playing the same trick on Malvolio. There is also a busy interchange of money and jewels, much of it carried by Viola. It reaches a climax when she is accused by Antonio of swindling him out of his purse, and Sir Toby, of all people, expresses righteous indignation.

But there is something clearly wrong with an account of the plot which sees nothing but a series of interlocking swindles. It is important to recognise that not all the deceptions are caused by human actions. The initial shipwreck which brings Viola and Sebastian separately to Illyria belongs to a category of events which can be found not only in Roman comedy but also in romance. The sea was so strongly associated with the idea of fate that in the Italian theatre a backdrop representing a stormy sea was called a *fortuna*. What the sea and Fortune have in common is randomness; this is why the goddess Fortune is depicted as blind, or blindfolded, and why Sebastian speaks of 'the blind waves and surges' which have 'devoured' his sister [v i 226]. The opposite of Fortune is Divine Providence (the word means fore*seeing*). When Sebastian realises that his sister is alive, he realises also that Olivia has been mistaking him for her. But he now sees events in a new light:

> So comes it, lady, you have been mistook.
> But nature to her bias drew in that.
> You would have been contracted to a maid.
> Nor are you therefore, by my life, deceived:
> You are betrothed both to a maid and man.          [v i 256–60]

Olivia may have been mistaken, but she was not deceived; there was a purpose in what happened, after all.

The characters are often confused as to whether they are the victims of human trickery or cosmic purpose. Malvolio in soliloquy says that 'All is fortune', and later, in an attempt at humility, thanks 'Jove', not his own merit, for the happiness offered him in the forged letter. In fact, he is the victim of purely human deception. On the other hand, Antonio thinks himself the victim of Sebastian's trickery, when it is mere chance that has led him to address himself to the wrong twin. Fears of witchcraft, demonic possession, and ghosts turn out in the end to have a rational explanation. But there remains a sense of something irrational, and mostly beneficent, behind the workings of the plot.

It is also important to remember that the plot is a love story. All the named characters except the enigmatic Fabian experience some form of love – at least, assuming that Sir Andrew knows what he is talking about when he offers Feste money for his 'leman'. Yet this love is taken for granted rather than explored. The play contains no straightforward love scenes. Though four men are suitors to Olivia, none of them woos her directly; two of them (Orsino and Sir Andrew) never speak to her at all until the final scene. Most of the characters, apart from Olivia and Sebastian, fall in love offstage, which is where the whole of Sir Toby's courtship of Maria takes place. The closest thing to a simple expression of feeling is Antonio's affection for Sebastian. Because of Viola's disguise, her scenes with Orsino and Olivia must necessarily consist of indirect, or misdirected, statements about love. This style is taken to its absurd extreme in Maria's letter to Malvolio and his wooing of Olivia. The fact that both are expressed in riddles prolongs the misunderstanding – and the joke.

If we look only at what is *said* in the play, then, the characters' relationships seem to develop and alter at breakneck speed, in accordance with Feste's image of 'the whirligig of time' [v i 374]. Insofar as the play is a play of intrigue, it requires this speed. One reason why Latin and Italian comedies normally take place within a single day is that most of their deceptions could not plausibly succeed if anyone were given time to think. Maria is aware, once Malvolio has appeared in his yellow stockings, that time is short: 'Nay, pursue him now, lest the device take air, and taint' [III iv 130–1]. *Twelfth Night,* in this time scheme, stands for the compression of time which seems to occur on a holiday; the events of the play cannot possibly occur within a single night, but it feels as if they did.

But, as Rosalind says in *As You Like It,* 'Time travels in divers paces with divers persons' [III ii 290–1]. *Twelfth Night* contains several references to clocks and watches, and two specific references to the passage of time: Viola has been in Orsino's service three weeks by the beginning of I iv, and three months by the beginning of v i. Theirs is a relationship which requires time for its maturing, and their language takes this into account. Even in her first scene Viola does not want to be known until she can make 'mine own occasion mellow' [I ii 44]; in her soliloquy in II ii, she recognises that the three-way stalemate between herself and Orsino and Olivia can be ended only by time; and Orsino at last speaks of their marriage as something that will happen when 'golden time convents' [v i 379]. His phrase suggests that the whirligig of the Malvolio plot has been spinning within a more gradual and spacious process, such as is needed to make the characters' marriages emotionally as well as dramatically satisfying. Shakespeare may be making a joke about the two time-schemes when Malvolio chases after Viola in the street:

> MAL.   Were not you even now with the Countess Olivia?
> VIOLA  Even now, sir; on a moderate pace I have since arrived but
>        hither.                                              [II ii 1–4]

Between Viola's departure from Olivia's house and Malvolio's catching up with her, we have watched a whole scene between Sebastian and Antonio. Malvolio has certainly taken his time on the way – there is a stage tradition (see J. C. Trewin, *Going to Shakespeare,* 1978, p. 165) that he gasps with horror when Olivia tells him to 'Run' – but Viola's line may also be a comic acknowledgement that time has virtually stood still since I v.

The concept of holiday, to some extent, reconciles the two time-schemes. Holidays are slaves to time, tied to particular dates and limited in duration, but they are also outside time, in that their ritualistic overturning of custom allows things to happen which would otherwise require a long period of preparation. Much research has been done on the festival tradition that lies behind Twelfth Night customs: the Lord of Misrule, the Feast of Fools, the gift-giving which paralleled that of the three kings whose visit to the Christ Child is commemorated on 6 January. The Christmas holiday season took over from the Roman Saturnalia a number of customs which permitted licensed irreverence through disguisings, parodies of solemn events, and reversals of roles between men and women, masters and servants, clergy and laity. L. G. Salingar has summed up this aspect of *Twelfth Night*:

> The sub-plot shows a prolonged season of misrule, or 'uncivil rule',
> in Olivia's household, with Sir Toby turning night into day; there
> are drinking, dancing and singing, scenes of mock wooing, a mock
> sword fight, and the gulling of an unpopular member of the
> household, with Feste mumming it as a priest and attempting a
> mock exorcism in the manner of the Feast of Fools. . . . A girl and a
> coward are given out to be ferocious duellists; a steward imagines
> that he can marry his lady; and finally a fool pretends to a wise man
> that darkness is light
>
> ('The Design of *Twelfth Night*', *Shakespeare Quarterly*, 9
> (1958) p. 118)

Feste's mock exorcism of Malvolio inverts the proper role of the priest; while pretending to test his parishioner's orthodoxy, he actually tries to convert him to a heresy and insists, 'Thou shalt hold the opinion of Pythagoras ere I will allow of thy wits' [IV ii 56–8]. Maria has already compared the steward's faith in her forged letter to the fanaticism of a heretic, 'for there is no Christian, that means to be saved by believing rightly, can ever believe such impossible passages of grossness' [III ii 65–9]. But Olivia has said the same of the 'text' on which Viola offered to preach: that is, Orsino's love for her [I v 211–18]; the clichés of love, which make the loved one an object of worship, are thus related to the parody of religious ritual.

The conflict between Malvolio and the others probably owes something to topical factors. The branch of Protestantism known as Puritanism believed that the church, and society at large, should be 'purified' of customs which had no biblical justification and which, over the years, had become the excuse for rowdiness. It is possible that Sir Toby and Feste are meant to be of an older generation than Malvolio. Feste is said to be 'one that the Lady Olivia's father took much delight in' [II iv 11–12], and she herself says that his 'fooling grows old' [I v 105]. But there must always have been tension between the forces of order and those of holiday. As C. L. Barber says, Malvolio 'is not hostile to holiday because he is a Puritan; he is like a Puritan because he is hostile to holiday' (*Shakespeare's Festive Comedy*, 1959, p. 256). Shakespeare makes fun of Sir Andrew's mindless prejudice against Puritanism ('I have no exquisite reason for't, but I have reason good enough' [II iii 138–9]), and makes it clear that Maria's dislike of Malvolio is based on his self-love rather than his religious attitude.

If Malvolio is only *like* a Puritan, *Twelfth Night* is perhaps only *like* a holiday. None of the characters seems to think of the revelry as being justified by the season. There are mentions of 'the twelfth day of December' [II iii 83], 'mid-summer madness' [III iv 56] and 'More matter for a May morning' [III iv 141]; Sir Andrew also suggests that he and Toby should 'set about some revels' [I iii 128]. But when Malvolio complains about their lack of respect for 'place, persons nor time' [II iii 90], they do not point out that the time *is* appropriate for song and dance. Instead, Toby retorts 'We did keep time, sir, in our catches' [92]. In *As You Like It*, Touchstone makes a similar pun on musical time as opposed to 'real' time; one of the boy singers insists 'we kept time, we lost not our time', and he replies 'By my troth, yes; I count it but time lost to hear such a foolish song' [v iii 34–7]. In *Twelfth Night*, the Fool is himself a singer, and the joke is reversed. Olivia sees Feste's fooling as time-wasting, something she indulges 'for want of other idleness' [I v 59], and those characters who sit listening to his songs and his nonsense patter are undoubtedly wasting time, doing nothing. Yet they also achieve, through the music, a wordless communion which goes deeper than anything they can say to one another. This is true not only of Orsino and Viola during the singing of 'Come Away Death', but of the almost inarticulate reactions of the two drunken knights:

> SIR AND.   Excellent good, i'faith.
> SIR TOBY   Good, good.                                    [II iii 43–4]

Feste uses his fooling, in his first Scene, to warn Olivia against wasting her youth in mourning 'your brother's soul, being in heaven' [I v 65–6]; Malvolio, asked his opinion of this fooling, replies that Feste will get better and better at it 'till the pangs of death shake him' [70–1]. The two ideas of *carpe diem* – seize the day – and *memento mori* – remember that you must die – come together most memorably in Feste's song:

> Then come kiss me, sweet and twenty,
> Youth's a stuff will not endure.                        [II iii 49–50]

And Olivia declares her love for Cesario, swearing by the shortlived 'roses of the spring', in a scene where the sound of a clock striking has reminded her of 'the waste of time'. These reminders of the passing of time are appropriate to a play whose title evokes not just the holiday season but the *last* night of that season.


## 3   PATTERNS OF LANGUAGE AND ACTION


At one point in *Gl'Ingannati* – one of the Italian comedies involving a disguised girl – a party of travellers arrives in town and has to choose between two rival inns, The Mirror and The Fool (or, in another translation, The Madman). It is obvious from the other puns in this dialogue that, when the party finally decides to stay at The Fool, their choice has an ironic significance. It is the more ironic, because one member of the party is the heroine's long-lost brother. The play thus neatly makes its dramatic point: until everyone recognises that brother and sister are mirror images, the situation is going to make fools of them all.

This is a comparatively simple example of the way in which the mistaken identity plot can attract other kinds of double meanings and symmetrical patterns. The patterns in *Twelfth Night* also reinforce its theme. They are not likely to be noticed at a first reading, though they can be brought out more clearly in a production, but they contribute to the sense of satisfaction which is present at the end of the play.

The plot device of the twins who are both identical and different belongs to a pattern of associations which Shakespeare and his contemporaries absorbed from one of the best-loved Latin poems of the period, Ovid's *Metamorphoses*. Ovid's interlocking stories merge into each other just as their subjects do; he tells of transformations from one state into another, sometimes caused by an external force and sometimes by the power of an emotion. Sometimes the metamorphosis is destructive rather than regenerative. The puns on 'hart' and 'heart', used by both Orsino and Olivia when they are in love, suggest the story of Acteon, a huntsman who was literally 'changed into a hart' and torn to pieces by his hounds. Samuel Johnson's edition explains that he 'represents a man who, indulging his eyes, or his imagination, with the view of a woman that he cannot gain, has his heart torn with incessant longing'. Another legend about sterile, unfulfilled love is that of Echo, the nymph who pined away with vain love for the selfish youth Narcissus; as punishment for his self-love he finally wasted away with longing for his own reflection and became a daffodil. D. J. Palmer has shown in his essay '*Twelfth Night* and the Myth of Echo and Narcissus' (*Shakespeare Survey 32*), the relation of this legend to the play's castigation of self-love and the insistence that love must be returned – or echoed – if it is to be meaningful.

There is a difference, however, between responding and merely repeating. The static and hopeless nature of Orsino's love for Olivia and hers for Cesario appears in their reiteration of the same actions: Orsino is twice seen urging Cesario to go 'once more' to the Countess; she is twice seen pleading with

Cesario to love her or at least to 'come again'. In i i, Orsino asks for the repetition of a musical phrase with a 'dying fall', in ii iv, he asks for the repetition of a song about death which he heard the previous night. Olivia refers to his suit to her as 'the old tune', and compares it to howling after music: repetition of the same notes, corresponding to his endless hunting after an unattainable object.

Another kind of echo, however, suggests a genuine reciprocation of feeling between characters. The relationship between Orsino and Viola is created, to a large extent, by her ability to enter into his language. The cadence of her lines in i ii –

> And what should I do in Illyria?
> My brother, he is in Elysium.                        [3–4]

– has the sweetness, and the dying fall, which he had sought in the music of i i. In ii iv, when he asks, 'How dost thou like this tune?', he is struck by her reply:

> VIOLA   It gives a very echo to the seat
>               Where love is throned.
> ORSINO  Thou dost speak masterly.                [17–20]

It is not surprising that he finds her speech 'masterly'; he has already used the same image himself, when he looked forward to a time when Olivia's

> . . . liver, brain and heart,
> Those sovereign thrones, are all supplied and filled –
> Her sweet perfections – with one self king!        [i i 38–40]

The 'king' to whom he refers is primarily Love (as Viola's speech shows), but there is a further suggestion that it may be Orsino himself. His wish is fulfilled in Viola's making him her 'lord' while she acts as his servant, and at the end, when she becomes her 'master's mistress', he also addresses her as 'Orsino's mistress, and his fancy's queen' [v i 385]. This line has sometimes been taken to show that Orsino has learned nothing in the course of the play, since he repeats the suspect word 'fancy', rather than 'love', from the opening scene. But in the context of the other lines quoted here it can also be seen as a development of feeling. Its main effect, however, is to suggest yet again the subtle affinity between him and Viola.

The 'willow cabin' speech is the most complex illustration of the way in which an echo can also be a metamorphosis. Throughout this scene, Cesario claims to be repeating what he has 'studied' (memorised), true to Orsino's instruction 'to act my woes'. And the speech does, in fact, represent a metamorphosis of Orsino's own words. He had already told Cesario:

> Be not denied access; stand at her doors,
> And tell them, there thy fixed foot shall grow
> Till thou have audience. . . .
> Be clamorous and leap all civil bounds
> Rather than make unprofited return.     [I iv 16–18, 21–2]

The idea that Viola should threaten to grow to the spot suggests a joke about metamorphosis to a tree. What she actually says on arrival, is relayed by Malvolio: 'he says he'll stand at your door like a sheriff's post and be the supporter to a bench, but he'll speak with you' [I v 142–4]. It is interesting to note that Malvolio is another character who is said to be able to speak only what he has 'studied': according to Maria, he 'cons state without book and utters it by great swathes' [II iii 141–2]. The dryness of his speech, and the sense he gives that every sentence knows where it is going to end, are another example of uncreative repetition. Even in his final scene, where he is given one speech of verse [v i 328–42], it is abstract, rhetorical, a series of repeated 'why's.

Viola, however, both retains and transcends the image from which she started, that of the absurdly persistent suitor:

> OLIVIA    Why, what would you?
> VIOLA     Make me a willow cabin at your gate,
>        And call upon my soul within the house;
>        Write loyal cantons of contemned love
>        And sing them loud even in the dead of night;
>        Hallow your name to the reverberate hills
>        And make the babbling gossip of the air
>        Cry out 'Olivia!' O, you should not rest
>        Between the elements of air and earth,
>        But you should pity me.       [I v 257–65]

What Viola has done is to exaggerate still further the sense of desperate determination which her master has impressed on her. Instead of merely wearing a willow garland, as forsaken lovers traditionally did, she proposes to build a whole cabin of it; instead of merely singing, she will sing 'loud' and 'in the dead of night'. (When Sir Toby, Feste and Sir Andrew put this suggestion into practice in II iii, Olivia promptly asks Malvolio to turn them out.) Echo herself becomes only a 'babbling gossip'. Yet the speech is shot through with feeling. Some of this results from the context: the audience already knows of Viola's love for Orsino, which she will not be able to shout out until the end of the play, and her imaginative entering into his feelings is set off against the element of parody. 'Hallow' is a key word here. In the sense of 'halloo' or shout, it represents the clamour which Orsino had recommended; in the sense of 'make holy', it recalls Sonnet 108 ('Even as when first I hallowed thy fair name') which is almost blasphemous in its adoration.

Other verbal patterns are used more openly. Feste often comments on odd turns of phrase; Sir Andrew tries to imitate them. Words and phrases are handed from speaker to speaker, as are the three letters which are read aloud during the play. The falseness of words, on which Feste remarks in III i, is particularly evident in Malvolio's letter, which sounds like that of a madman when Feste begins to read it, and 'savours not much of distraction' in Fabian's rendering [v i 311]. Feste's repetition of Malvolio's earlier phrases, in his final speech, reminds him of the poetic justice in his metamorphosis from a man who never laughed at fools to a 'poor fool', as Olivia calls him [v i 367], at whom everyone laughs.

More visible kinds of pattern include the entrances and exits of the characters, their grouping, and the alternation of a full stage with a nearly empty one. While some of these things are left for the director to arrange, others are implicit in the way the play is structured. Emrys Jones has analysed the 'shape' of II v:

> First the three dupers enter; then, briefly, Maria; lastly Malvolio. The main business of the scene follows. Malvolio leaves the stage to the dupers again, who are again joined by Maria, before they too

leave. Such a sequence organizes a kind of dramatic space. We
approach it, we enter it, and we emerge from it. Or we can see it as a
pyramid: the dupers are on stage throughout, and Malvolio comes
on and goes off, leaving them still there. Just before he comes and
just after he goes, Maria appears. Shakespeare seems to use her to
demarcate the central dramatic space formed by the scene.
Without her two brief appearances the scene would feel less elegant
a shape in our minds.

(*Scenic Form in Shakespeare*, 1971, p. 25)

The earlier scene with these characters, II iii, has a similar
shape, though it is not clear when or whether Feste is meant to
leave. But its form is made clear by verbal means as well: it
opens with Sir Toby claiming that being up after midnight
means being up early, and it ends with his claiming that it is
now 'too late to go to bed'.

If the play was written for a stage with two doors at the back
(as was the case in the Middle Temple hall, and seems to have
been the case at the Globe), the entrances and exits would have
been particularly noticeable; it has been estimated that the
doors at the Globe were 27 feet from the front of the stage.
*Twelfth Night* is unusual in the amount of attention that is paid
to the business of getting in and out of these doors. All through
the first act, the emphasis is on the difficulty of entering Olivia's
house, not only for Orsino's emissaries but even for members of
the household. Act I, scene iii opens with Maria letting Toby
in, while in I v she is letting Feste in – in each case, with a
warning about their behaviour. Viola has to run a gauntlet
consisting of Maria, Sir Toby and Malvolio. A great deal of her
part consists in walking briskly in and out of doors 'between
this lady and this lord' [v i 255].

The juxtaposition of entrances and exits – quite different
from the use of curtains or lighting to create a new scene –
allowed for special kinds of dramatic effect. Skilful use of the
two doors could allow one set of characters to disappear at one
door behind the procession of new characters who were coming
on through the other. Or a character could make a feature of his
exit, starting to go off and then returning with an afterthought,
as Malvolio seems to do in II v. Sebastian's entrances are

particularly interesting. His first one comes just after Olivia has sent Malvolio to overtake Cesario. We are thus expecting the page to reappear, and it is possible that the audience was meant to be deceived at the first entrance of the other twin. In IV iii, Sebastian enters declaring 'This is the air, that is the glorious sun' immediately after Malvolio's 'dark house' scene. The words almost create a lighting change, such as most modern directors introduce at this point.

The motive for these metamorphoses, patterns and pairings is not simply a love of complex design, though Shakespeare, like his contemporaries, certainly *did* love it. 'Journeys end in lovers meeting', Feste sings, and *Twelfth Night* belongs to a category of play in which a real purpose turns out to underlie the apparently random nature of events. Shakespeare stresses the randomness at the beginning, with an unusually abrupt series of brief scenes: only Olivia's name is mentioned in I i; we learn Orsino's name in I ii; in I iii we deduce that Toby's 'niece' and 'the count' must be this same Olivia and Orsino. Viola does not acquire a name until the last scene of the play. In the nineteenth century it was common practice to reverse the order of I i and I ii, and one production even began with II i, the conversation between Antonio and Sebastian, in order to get the facts of the shipwreck and the brother–sister resemblance explained in a forthright manner. It would appear, however, that Shake-speare wished to begin with the characters as isolated as possible from one another. He emphasises the difficulty of access to Olivia by mentioning her in the first four scenes but making the audience wait until I v for her first entrance. In her subsequent scenes there are references to outdoor scenery which suggest that she is becoming less like the 'cloistress' in a 'chamber' who was described in I i. In the last act, she finally comes out of her house, and this enables a series of confrontations to take place, leading first to confusion and accusations of insanity, then to a re-establishing of order.

## 4 CLOSE ANALYSIS: ACT V, SCENE i

By contrast with the short scenes of Act I, Shakespeare ends the play with a single scene in which the delicate balance and symmetry of his design is particularly well illustrated. The brief discussion of 'his letter' (the audience guesses whose) between Feste and Fabian indicates that a resolution of Malvolio's predicament is within sight, but it is postponed by the entrance of Orsino and Viola. The subplot thus acts as a framework for the resolution of the main plot, which is itself promised and then postponed. Each new entrance brings an additional complication in the form of a new accusation against Cesario. Antonio accuses him of cowardice and ingratitude, Olivia of deceit and cowardice; the priest testifies to the marriage of Cesario and Olivia, thus apparently proving the page a liar; Sir Andrew and Sir Toby give visible proof that he is also a thug.

According to the director's choice, this can be either the tensest or the funniest part of the play. From the point of view of any one of the characters, the situation is desperate. It is particularly desperate for Viola, since she seems about to lose Orsino forever. At the same time, there are several factors which should keep the audience from taking her predicament too seriously. For one thing, everyone knows that Sebastian must be somewhere in the vicinity; the skill of the playwright lies in distracting attention from this fact, through a series of interruptions, so that his arrival can both surprise and fulfil audience expectations. The other thing that defuses the melodrama is the ridiculously contradictory nature of the various accusations. Cesario has apparently managed to display disgraceful cowardice towards Orsino, Olivia and Antonio, yet to be 'the very devil incardinate' with the two knights. 'We took him for a coward', Sir Andrew says, bewildered. It is clear that Cesario is not the person that they – or anyone – took him for.

The alternation of verse and prose is another means by which Shakespeare controls the tone. Antonio's bitter sense of betrayal and Orsino's sudden jealousy are expressed in blank verse of great intensity. It is not clear what has given rise to

Orsino's anger, apart from Olivia's ostentatious demonstration
of favour towards Cesario. Nor is it clear whether Orsino is
merely meditating on the possibility of violence or is genuinely
on the verge of committing it. But the couplet into which he
drops at the end of his speech sets off a three-way rhyming
dialogue, the main effect of which is to draw attention to the
artificially tangled relationship of the speakers:

> ORSINO  . . . I'll sacrifice the lamb that I do love
> To spite a raven's heart within a dove.
> VIOLA  And I, most jocund, apt, and willingly
> To do you rest, a thousand deaths would die.
> OLIVIA  Where goes Cesario?
> VIOLA                    After him I love
> More than I love these eyes, more than my life,
> More, by all mores, than e'er I shall love wife.
>
> [v i 128–34]

The hyperbole of Orsino's images – lamb, raven, dove – is
matched by Viola's 'thousand deaths' and the 'mores' of her
second couplet, another example of her readiness to enter into
his emotional environment. Her unrhymed outcry, 'After him I
love', which releases her at last from the constraint of silence
('She never told her love') is made possible by Orsino's
unwitting declaration of his own feelings ('the lamb that I do
love'). But her speech then drops back into the riddling manner
which has characterised her scenes with Olivia; rhyme, in this
play, has been used most particularly for the moments when
Viola's double role has been emphasised. The broken lines of
the three-way exchange after Olivia has called Cesario 'husband' indicate the speed of events, but Olivia's awkward
inversion forces an awareness that the exchange is also in
rhyme.

> ORSINO  Husband?
> OLIVIA                    Ay, husband. Can he that deny?
> ORSINO  Her husband, sirrah?
> VIOLA                    No, my lord, not I.        [142–3]

A couplet divided among three speakers is a perfect formal

equivalent for the plot at this point: three characters are trying to form two couples.

The pace is slowed down, first by Olivia's speech in the 'norm' of blank verse, with its strange echo of the words she is supposed to have used to Malvolio ('Be not afraid of greatness'), and then by the priest, who delivers his evidence line by line, slowed down still further by the pause in one line and the elaborate parenthesis at the end. The effect can be comically slow, by contrast with the impatience of the other characters. Or, as John Russell Brown has pointed out (*Shakespeare's Plays in Performance*, 1979, p. 226), the speech can 'restore a sense of awe, an awareness of general and timeless implications', to the hectic scene.

Sometimes, since there is nothing further for him to do, the priest goes off again at the end of his speech, blissfully unaware of the consternation he is leaving behind him. Sometimes, as in Peter Hall's 1958 RSC production, he is still there when Malvolio complains of being visited by him (that is, Sir Topas), and reacts accordingly. At any rate, his speech ends with an incomplete line, which is completed, probably, by a pause in which everyone stares at the wretched Cesario. Orsino's contemptuous rejection brings a return of the rhyming couplets; he and Olivia seem united, for the first time in the play, by their mutual sense of injury.

The couplets establish the artificial comedy atmosphere for just long enough to make Sir Andrew's interruption a shock. It can be even more shocking if, as sometimes happens in contemporary productions, he arrives covered in blood and on the verge of a nervous breakdown. But even if he is more frightened than hurt, there may be the sense of the breaking of what one has taken to be an unwritten law: that comic characters do not bleed. Even in tragedy, there is a similar effect in the deaths of Mercutio in *Romeo and Juliet* and Roderigo in *Othello*.

But the most obvious effect is a lowering of the emotional temperature. Though Viola clings to blank verse as she must have clung to the ship in the storm, Orsino and Olivia are obliged to come down to Sir Andrew's level, to take command of the situation, and pretend that the activities of the notorious Cesario are of no concern to them personally. At this point a number of cross-currents meet, and a good production should allow them all to become apparent. It is, for example, the first time that Olivia and Sir Andrew, her supposed suitor, have ever exchanged words in the play. Though the line 'I had rather than forty pound I were at home' [line 175] suggests that Andrew may have been cured of his ambitions towards Olivia, there is still room for him to establish some sense of a relationship. An obvious comic effect is also written into 'Od's lifelings, here he is!' [181], which represents his first sight of Cesario, presumably masked until then behind the other characters. The extent of his astonishment will surprise the others, but not the audience, who realise that the knight had just left Cesario, as he thought, behind him.

Despite all the confusion, this entrance is also the beginning of the denouement, since Sir Andrew's 'and that I did, I was set on to do't by Sir Toby' [182–3] is as close as anyone ever gets to an explanation of the duel scene. But his exchange of accusations with Viola is comically at cross-purposes, since she is talking about the events of III iv and he about those of IV i. A further piece of untying is accomplished by Sir Toby when he calls Sir Andrew a gull; while the fact of Sir Andrew's stupidity is no revelation to anyone (not even Sir Andrew), Sir Toby's words do reveal the true nature of his supposed friendship and to that extent are also part of the denouement.

Stage drunkenness, like stage madness, allows a large amount of free association, and many of Sir Toby's lines recapitulate what has gone before. The odd reference to 'a passy-measures pavin' (a slow dance) recalls his speech about various dances in I iii, and may also apply to the slow gait with which he and his companion depart, so different from their capering in the earlier scene. The fact that he turns on Sir Andrew, for whom the one sure thing remaining in life was Sir Toby's friendship, used to be glossed over in the theatre because it seemed out of keeping with the comic tone of their roles. Now it is more likely to be played for pathos, but as Sir Andrew is given no lines it is not clear how far his eyes have been opened. His reaction could be anything from an inane giggle to a silent, deeply wounded departure by a different door from Toby's.

Normally, Sebastian enters at one door as the two knights and their helpers (usually Fabian and Feste – and Maria, though the text of the play does not mention her) are going out at the other. From his first line, 'I am sorry, madam, I have hurt your kinsman' [206], it seems likely that he has seen their departure, and he may be meant to arrive in the midst of the other characters before they are aware of him. But a director may prefer to hold his entrance until the others have gone, and have all eyes on him as he makes his apparently magical appearance. Not only is this entrance perfectly timed, his speech neatly counters two of the chief accusations against Viola, by making it immediately clear that it was he who fought with the two knights and married Olivia; his next lines, to Antonio, dispose of the accusation of ingratitude. He also re-establishes the romantic tone. Olivia's 'Get him to bed and let his hurt be looked to' [205] had already moved back to verse after the mainly prose interruption; Sebastian picks up the loose rhythm and continues to speak in it, but gradually modulates to the more lyrical tone of

> Pardon me, sweet one, even for the vows
> We made each other but so late ago. [211–12]

Still more important is the fact that he has gone straight to Olivia and has no eyes for anyone else. The following speeches build upon the atmosphere which has been thus created, making possible the strangely tentative reunion of brother and sister and the recognition of all the characters that the experience that has just united them is, and is not, magic.

Unlike most Shakespearean denouements, in which everyone who matters learns what has been going on, *Twelfth Night* leaves many of its characters as separate and isolated at the end as at the beginning, despite their brief intersection with other lives. Thus, Sir Andrew, Sir Toby and Malvolio do not know that Olivia has married Sebastian, or that Viola is Cesario; Maria, apparently, does not appear in the scene at all, and her marriage to Sir Toby is explained in what seems almost a throwaway line. No lines are provided for Fabian and Feste to take account of these facts, though, if they go offstage with the two knights, they presumably take in the implications of the scene when they return, and Fabian speaks of 'this present hour, / Which I have wondered at' [355–6]. Malvolio's release from prison comes almost by chance, as an obviously dragged-in mention of Viola's Sea Captain leads to Olivia's being reminded of his existence. His entry makes a long, uncomfortable interruption in the movement towards a happy ending. One reason it is so long is that, unlike other parts of the plot, the trick played on him *is* fully explained, first from his point of view, then from Olivia's, then from Fabian's, and finally from Feste's. Feste's speech is almost a musical recapitulation of themes from earlier parts of the play, including words spoken in scenes where he was not present. It is as if Shakespeare wished to counterpoint the mysterious, poetic feeling of the Viola–Sebastian story with a scene in which everything is nailed down and given an explanation in terms of human cleverness and moral justice. Orsino and Viola, Olivia and Sebastian, pick up one another's poetic language, whereas Malvolio and Feste simply repeat the very words of the forged letter which has been taken so literally.

Granville-Barker, who directed a famous *Twelfth Night* in 1912, called this final scene 'scandalously ill-arranged and ill-written . . . , the despair of any stage manager' (Director's Preface to Acting Edition). It has sometimes been rearranged to allow Viola to change back into her woman's clothes during Malvolio's scene and exchange vows of love with Orsino at the end. Many directors have also brought Maria onstage to look after Sir Toby. Terry Hands (RSC, 1979) had her and the two knights remain onstage until the end, so that they, like Antonio, could watch the happiness which they were unable to share. While it took an obvious liberty with the text, the presence of so many silent observers did not seem incongruous in performance. This is because the scene requires many of its characters to remain silent for long periods, while another part of the plot is being sorted out. It is possible to defend this apparently undramatic stagecraft. Like the gaps between scenes, the gaps within scenes can be valuable for actors who have to establish, or re-establish, a complex relationship in a short space of time.

We do not know precisely where Malvolio is going when he walks offstage, but by the time the other characters go out, the door has become the door of Olivia's house – once so hard to enter – into which they are all invited. The pattern is complete, as L. G. Salingar points out: 'At the beginning of the comedy, Olivia had mourned a brother, while Orsino resented it; at the end, she finds a brother again, in Orsino himself' ('The Design of *Twelfth Night*', p. 132). Some directors have emphasised the elements in the scene which do not fit the pattern, such as Antonio's silent presence; Feste has sometimes been sent off into the auditorium or the wind and the rain. But, whatever we are meant to imagine of Feste the character, at the end of his song the singer turns himself back into a performer – not a solitary figure, but a member of a company of actors who 'strive to please you every day' – and it is reasonable to suppose that he goes off to join them.

## 5   A Play for Actors

The last lines of Feste's song remind us that, for actors, work is play and play is work: their 'play' is done, but they 'strive' to please us every day. This fact would have been more obvious to the original spectators, since, before the first professional theatres were opened in 1576, it was only during holidays that plays were normally put on. Even in Shakespeare's time, this was still true of performances at Court and other special venues, like the Middle Temple.

Leslie Hotson suggests, in *The First Night of 'Twelfth Night'* (1954), that the entire play arose out of a specific holiday occasion. A distinguished Italian visitor to England, Virginio Orsino, attended a performance of an unnamed play at Whitehall, in the presence of the Queen, on Twelfth Night,

1601. Hotson argues that *Twelfth Night* was that play, that it
was written with Orsino's visit in mind, that one of the
characters was named in compliment to him, while Olivia was
a compliment to the Queen herself (olives being a symbol of
peace and thus appropriate to her reign), and that the Malvolio
plot was a joke at the expense of the Controller of the Queen's
Household. There are many arguments against this interpretation, not least that it is difficult to see how the Orsino–Olivia
story could have flattered either the real Orsino, who was
twenty-eight and married, or the Queen, who was sixty-seven
and antipathetic to marriage.

A more likely influence on the play is the Middle Temple
performance. Fabian is sometimes played as a law student
(notice his sage advice to Sir Andrew in III iv), and the
last-minute decision to include such a character might account
for his abrupt, unexplained appearance in the play. The
audience seems to be expected to know who he is without being
told, and he plays a number of his lines to them. It is tempting
to think that Shakespeare wrote the part in the first instance for
a special guest appearance by one of the law students, a link
between the professional actors and the amateur revellers who
were watching them. Tempting, but pointless. We know very
little about the original casting of *Twelfth Night*. It is possible,
however, that some features of the play may be due to the
circumstances of the Lord Chamberlain's men at the time of its
writing.

In the early years of the seventeenth century, as can be seen
from a famous passage in *Hamlet* [II ii 327–58], the companies of
child actors were at the height of their popularity, representing
serious competition for their adult rivals. Many of the boys in
these companies had started as choristers, and one source of
their appeal was the quality of the music in their productions.
In *Twelfth Night* Shakespeare may have been trying to beat
them at their own game. Though his earlier comedies contain
songs, these are given to professional singers, both boys and
adults, who have very few lines to speak. In *Twelfth Night* all the
songs are taken by adults, in character. The catch sung by Sir
Toby, Sir Andrew and Feste may have been meant to rival, or

parody, the part-songs of the children's plays, which 'usually celebrate festive revelry, proclaim the singers' animal appetites, and ridicule figures of authority' (Michael Shapiro, *Children of the Revels*, 1977, p. 240). Shakespeare has written the scene so that it will work equally well whether or not the actors playing Toby and Andrew are able to sing. If they are, so much the better; if not, Maria's and Malvolio's complaints will seem all the more justified.

Feste, on the other hand, *must* be able to sing. He has four solos as well as his part in the catch and other snatches of song in II iii. Unlike Amiens in *As You Like It*, he must also be able to perform comic patter, do impersonations, and sustain a virtuoso dialogue with himself in two voices. This last exercise [IV ii] is so difficult to bring off that many modern actors play only a shortened version of the scene. It looks as if it was written for an actor of special gifts, who was probably allowed to improvise at this point. It has been plausibly suggested that the actor in question was Robert Armin, who joined the Lord Chamberlain's Men in about 1599 as a replacement for their former clown, Will Kemp.

There are clues as to the physique of some of the actors. Maria was obviously the smallest of the boys – hence the jokes about her as a 'giant' and 'the youngest wren of nine'. Sir Toby and Sir Andrew must be the Fat Man/Thin Man team so dear to comic writers. The best-known actor in the company was Richard Burbage, who created the major Shakespearean tragic roles. The fact that the part of Malvolio has so often been given to a star actor does not necessarily mean that Burbage would have taken it, rather than Sir Toby or Orsino, but it seems likely. For one thing, Malvolio's first entrance is remarkably similar to Hamlet's: both characters are on stage, in black, for some time before they speak, and have to be drawn forcibly into the conversation. This use of suspense is more intelligible if the part is being played by a star whose first line is eagerly awaited. (The relative dates of *Hamlet* and *Twelfth Night* are not known; if the comedy were later than the tragedy, it could have been an opportunity for Burbage to parody his own performance. The yellow stockings, for example, are the focus of a mock mad

scene which can be compared with Ophelia's description of
Hamlet's behaviour to her.)

Another point which Hamlet and Malvolio have in common
is their dislike of clowns who get above themselves and steal
scenes. The animosity between Feste and Malvolio which
begins and ends their part of the plot is an effective theatrical
exploitation of what may have been a real problem. After the
drinking scene [II iii], which sets Malvolio and the comic
characters against each other, Shakespeare keeps a careful
division of dramatic attention between Feste and Malvolio.
The letter-reading scene [II v] is made Fool-proof through the
replacement of Feste by Fabian, whose job it is to keep the other
actors under control. But in the 'dark house', Malvolio is kept
out of sight 'within' (as the stage direction says), so that he
cannot distract from Feste's elaborate fooling. All the exuber-
ant comic scenes are similarly controlled. The drinking scene is
interrupted, first by Maria, then by Malvolio. The duel scene is
interrupted by Antonio. One theory is that Shakespeare played
this part himself, knowing what a meal the comedians would
make of the mock fight if they were not stopped in time. The
play's construction certainly suggests that he was aware of the
problems that resulted from putting several talented indi-
vidualists on stage together. But this pattern of wild comedy
followed by repression is not only a theatrical necessity; it also
reinforces the play's title, which implies that revelry must come
to an end.

Productions since Shakespeare's time have been under
different theatrical constraints and have reflected these in their
treatment of the play. The music probably suffered the most in
eighteenth- and nineteenth-century revivals. Though everyone
who sees the play notices how important the songs are for its
atmosphere, it would have been hard to discover this before the
twentieth century. In the eighteenth century, neither 'O
Mistress Mine' nor 'Come Away Death' was sung, and the
'Epilogue Song', as it was called, reappeared only in 1763,
when the actor playing Feste composed (or perhaps adapted)
the tune which is still most frequently used. (He also composed
an extra song for Olivia, which used to be sung after III i.) In the

drinking scene, the revellers always sang catches, though not the ones Shakespeare had prescribed. With the comic songs left in and the more romantic ones cut out, it is evident that the balance of the play, and Feste's part especially, would have been tipped towards the comic side. In nineteenth-century productions other songs of a more sentimental kind were added – there was even an operatic *Twelfth Night* in 1820 – but it was still possible for Bernard Shaw to complain in 1894 about the assumption that 'any song by Shakespeare is appropriate to any play written by him, except, perhaps, the play in which it appears' (*The World*, 24 Jan. 1894; repr. Edwin Wilson (ed.), *Shaw on Shakespeare*, 1961, p. 190).

Other evidence as to how the play was regarded in the eighteenth century can be found in the notes to *Bell's Edition of Shakespeare* (1773), which gives the text performed at Drury Lane and Covent Garden theatres. The commentator gives most of his praise to the second and third acts, which contain most of the Malvolio plot. In his notes on individual characters he forgot to mention Viola. Olivia, however, gets more attention than one might expect; the actress 'should be a very sensible [expressive] speaker, with an elegant figure and graceful deportment' (p. 327). It would appear that some actresses at least played the part as a comedy of manners heroine: in the play's first major revival, in 1741, Olivia was played by a popular comedienne, Kitty Clive; in 1822, Charles Lamb praised an actress of the late eighteenth century for catching 'the imperious fantastic humour of the character'.

Other notes in *Bell's Edition* place the comic characters firmly within established types: Sir Toby requires 'jollity of features, figure and expression'; Sir Andrew can resemble Slender in *The Merry Wives of Windsor*, and Feste can have precisely the same qualities as Touchstone in *As You Like It*. Malvolio should embody 'a dry coxcombly importance, quaintly expressed'. Interestingly, though the beauty of Orsino's opening lines is praised, the note adds that this character can be adequately played by 'a second rate actor'. All this corroborates what was suggested by the treatment of the music: in the theatre at least, people liked *Twelfth Night* mainly for its comic scenes.

Nevertheless, this edition praises the 'matchless picturesque beauty' of Viola's speech beginning 'She never told her love', and Haydn set these lines to music in 1792. In 1817, Hazlitt, in his influential *Characters of Shakespeare's Plays*, redirected critical emphasis towards the romance of the play: 'The great and secret charm of *Twelfth Night* is the character of Viola. Much as we like cakes and ale, there is something that we like better.'

The part of Viola was, of course, written for a boy; since 1660, it has been played by a woman. It is not easy to appreciate the importance of this fact for criticism of the character in both text and performance. Many of Shakespeare's female characters disguise themselves as boys: Portia and Nerissa in *The Merchant of Venice* and Rosalind in *As You Like It* enjoy their disguises and play up to them, whereas Julia in *The Two Gentlemen of Verona* and Imogen in *Cymbeline* are for the most part unhappy in disguise. Viola's attitude seems somewhat between the two, and there has been some disagreement as to whether or not she is, in Samuel Johnson's phrase (in his edition of 1765), 'a cunning schemer, never at a loss'. Even in 1811 a reviewer commented that 'the disguise of women in male attire . . . always strikes one as a gross violation of probability, especially if represented as accompanied with delicacy of mind' (Leigh Hunt, in Gāmini Salgādo (ed.), *Eyewitnesses of Shakespeare*, 1975, p. 205).

The reason why Viola's character posed such problems was simply that, until after the First World War, no period of female fashion allowed more than the ankle to be revealed; it was only in theatrical contexts – ballet, pantomime and 'breeches roles' like Viola's – that men had an opportunity to see women's legs. Thus, a device which in Shakespeare is presented as a means of preserving modesty was bound, in performance, to have the opposite effect. There seems good reason to believe that *Twelfth Night* owed its revival at Drury Lane in 1741 to the stunning success which the attractive Peg Woffington had just achieved in 'breeches roles' at a rival theatre (see Arthur Scouten, *The London Stage 1729–1747*, 1965, pt 3, vol. I, cl–cli). Drury Lane promptly put on, in quick succession, *As You Like It*, *Twelfth Night* and *The Merchant of Venice*.

Not everyone shared Johnson's view of Viola as an adventuress; Lamb gives a fine account of an actress who moved him with her delivery of the 'She never told her love' speech, 'thought springing up after thought, I would almost say, as they were watered by her tears' ('On Some of the Old Actors', *Essays of Elia*). But one can set beside this Leigh Hunt's review of an 1820 production which devotes itself to the leading lady's 'right feminine leg, delicate in foot, trim in ankle, and with a calf at once soft and well-cut, distinguished and unobtrusive' (Stanley Wells, 'Leigh Hunt's Theatre Criticism', *Essays and Studies*, 1980, p. 127). As late as 1888, in *The Henry Irving Shakespeare*, another theatre-orientated edition, the commentator notes that 'Viola must always prove an attractive impersonation to any young actress with an elegant figure'. In this context, it is difficult to see how any actress could really be more, in the eyes of the male spectators at least, than a pair of legs. The stress on her purity and melancholy seems an over-reaction to the embarrassment caused by her disguise. A similar insistence on sobriety had reduced the once lively figure of Olivia to a cipher, Orsino to a bore, and Sebastian to a non-entity. Thus, by 1901, Max Beerbohm could describe all four lovers as dancers in a quadrille, and argue that the play was redeemed only by its comic scenes (*More Theatres, 1898–1903*, 1969, pp. 346–8).

As Beerbohm's comment indicates, both Feste and Malvolio had been growing more and more important. The first thing that strikes one about eighteenth-century accounts of Feste is that he is not called Feste. He is listed simply as 'Clown' in the first cast list, which was added in the edition of 1709; his name is mentioned only once [ii iv 11] and he is never called by it either in the dialogue or the speech prefixes of the play. It was not until the nineteenth century that he was regarded as a person with a name rather than as a performer with a function. Jesters were popular characters in the drama and novels of the century, where interest usually focused on the tension between the comic mask and the human being beneath it. Beerbohm wrote approvingly of a Feste who infused 'a touch of sinistry into his mirth' (*More Theatres, 1898–1903*, 1969, p. 349). And

Gilbert and Sullivan's *Yeomen of the Guard* (1888) is probably to blame for the interpretation, at one time quite common in the theatre, which is described by the director of a 1922 production:

> Feste, of course, is in love with Olivia, his Mistress, though never daring to express it. At the close, as the characters *exeunt*, Feste, sitting by the arch, singing 'for the rain, it raineth every day', stooped swiftly and kissed the hem of Olivia's gown as she passed. One learned what a variety and depth of feeling can be expressed in a 'hey ho'.          (Norman McDermott, *Everymania*, 1975, p. 52)

The interpretation of Malvolio offers an interesting example of the interdependence of literary and theatrical criticism. Charles Lamb's 'Essay on Some of the Old Actors' (1822), in which he also mentions other performers of *Twelfth Night*, describes at some length the Malvolio of Robert Bensley, which he was remembering at a distance of some twenty years. Lamb was fully aware of the comic side of Bensley's impersonation – 'He was starch, spruce, opinionated' – but he also noted that 'his superstructure of pride seemed bottomed upon a sense of worth'. Lamb identified the character's delusions with those of Don Quixote, and his sympathy for what he took to be romantic idealism led him to read into the performance qualities which in all probability were not there. Thus, Malvolio's behaviour in II ii, which Viola describes as 'churlish', struck him as a 'careless committal of the ring to the ground' which 'bespeaks a generosity of birth and feeling'. When he goes on to write of the 'kind of tragic interest' which he felt for Malvolio in the latter part of the play, he is saying more about himself than about the way in which Bensley played the part, as has been made clear by scholars who have compared his account with those of other spectators. But the essay is a splendid piece of writing, and it has been suggested that it may have inspired the Malvolio of Henry Irving, who had never seen *Twelfth Night* when he played the part in his own production of 1884 (Sylvan Barnet, 'Charles Lamb and the Tragic Malvolio', *Shakespeare Quarterly*, 33, 1944).

Irving always liked to seek out the human qualities in the characters he played and, in projecting Malvolio's own view of himself ('Never was man thus wronged'), he was probably doing no more than many earlier actors. But, as manager of the Lyceum Theatre, he was in a position to build the entire production round his conception. The other comic characters were not strongly cast, to say the least: Feste could not sing, and Sir Toby and Sir Andrew managed not to raise a single laugh in their scenes. Only Ellen Terry, as Viola, was allowed to make anything of her role. Irving's conception started from Lamb's emphasis on the power of fantasy. He made his first entrance 'with nose in air and eyes half shut, as if with singular and moody contemplation' (Sir Edward Russell, quoted in *Variorum*, 1901, p. 400). Though he anticipated some modern interpretations by suggesting the character's low birth, he was so formidable that one critic apparently objected that Maria would never have dared to play that trick on such a man. It was in the letter-reading scene, however, that the nature of his design was clear. The fullest account is in a review by Edward Aveling:

> At the end of the scene his exit was not with a pompous swaggering strut, Malvolio passed out with his face buried in his hands, strangely moved, overwhelmed with his good fortune. Then we began to see what real pain this foolish jest of Maria was, like most foolish jests, to cause.
>
> (in Salgādo (ed.), *Eyewitnesses of Shakespeare*, p. 214)

The reviewer goes on to describe the horror of the 'dark room', which was in fact a prison: 'The mental and physical horror of darkness and the longing yearning for deliverance from a prison cell were never so realised, I think, before' (p. 215). He spoke his final revengeful line 'with the concentrated hate and ungovernable vehemence of a Shylock' (Clement Scott, quoted in *Variorum*, p. 402).

This interpretation was not much liked by the public, who preferred their *Twelfth Nights* to be funny, but it inspired a good deal of critical debate, some of which can be sampled in the appendix to Furness's *Variorum* (1901). Irving's distortion of the play drew attention to a side of it that had often been glossed over. Shakespeare did not apparently wish the audience to *see*

Malvolio 'in a dark room and bound' [III iv 134–5], but he did make it clear that this was Sir Toby's plan, and that the conspirators did briefly consider, and laugh at, the possibility that they might 'make him mad indeed' [132]. No director or critic since Irving has been able to ignore the disturbing implications of this part of the plot. The reviewer F. A. Marshall wrote that he had 'never thought Malvolio was so serious a character as Mr. Irving represented him', but, after rereading the play, he concluded that the actor had been right ('Our Play-Box', *The Theatre*, 1884). This illustrates the extent to which a powerful theatrical interpretation can colour one's reading. Some of the productions about to be discussed may be equally important for its critical history – not only in spite of, but even because of, their varying emphases.

# PART TWO: PERFORMANCE

## 6 INTRODUCTION

In this section, I shall be examining four productions in detail:

1. The RSC production, directed by John Barton, at Stratford-upon-Avon and the Aldwych Theatre, London, 1969–71. This went through a number of cast changes at its various revivals. The cast which I saw, at the Aldwych in 1970, included: Judi Dench as Viola, Lisa Harrow as Olivia, Elizabeth Spriggs as Maria, Richard Pasco as Orsino, Leslie Sands as Sir Toby Belch, Barrie Ingham as Sir Andrew Aguecheek, Emrys James as Feste, and Donald Sinden as Malvolio. The sets were by Christopher Morley, costumes by Stephanie Howard, lighting by Brian Harris and Christopher Morley, and music arranged by Michael Tubbs.

2. The RSC production, directed by Peter Gill, at Stratford-upon-Avon and the Aldwych, 1974–5. The production under discussion was that given at Stratford in 1974, with Jane Lapotaire as Viola, Mary Rutherford as Olivia, Patricia Hayes as Maria, John Price as Orsino, David Waller as Sir Toby Belch, Frank Thornton as Sir Andrew Aguecheek, Ron Pember as Feste, and Nicol Williamson as Malvolio. The sets were by William Dudley, costumes by Deirdre Clancy, music by George Fenton, and lighting by Rory Dempster.

3. The Haymarket Theatre, Leicester, production directed by Robin Midgley, 1979: Pippa Guard as Viola, Joanne Pearce as Olivia, Pamela Cundell as Maria, Malcolm Sinclair as Orsino, James Hayter as Sir Toby Belch, Robert Bridges as Sir Andrew Aguecheek, Roy Macready as Feste, and Peter Copley as Malvolio. The sets were by Adrian Vaux, lighting by Chris Ellis, and musical direction by Ian Smith.

4. The Berkeley Shakespeare Festival, directed by Julian Lopez-Morillas, 1981–2: Joan Mankin as Viola, Stacey Cole as

Olivia, Marilyn Prince as Maria, Kevin Gardiner as Orsino, Robert Sinclair as Sir Toby Belch, Charles Martinet as Sir Andrew Aguecheek, Drew Lubarsky as Feste, and Paul Vincent O'Connor as Malvolio. Sets were by Warren Travis, lighting by Margaret Anne Dunn, and musical direction by Mitchell Sandler.

In the case of the two RSC productions, it has been possible to draw on the extensive archives of the Shakespeare Centre in Stratford; I have examined promptbooks for the productions of 1958, 1971 (the other promptbooks of the Barton production having disappeared), 1974 and 1979, as well as press cuttings for all productions since 1958. A very full description of the Barton *Twelfth Night* – with which I have tried to avoid excessive overlapping – is in Stanley Wells, *Royal Shakespeare* (1976). He calls his account 'a composite one', and, in the case of the two RSC productions, the same will be true of mine.

No other theatre is so well documented as the RST. In attempting to refresh my memory of the Leicester production I have benefited from discussion with the director, Robin Midgley, who also made available his collection of production photographs and press cuttings. For the Berkeley production, I have drawn on the notes which I took at the time. Where no source is given for a statement in this section, I am drawing either on my own recollections or on those of others to whom I have talked.

An experienced amateur actor who has played Sir Andrew Aguecheek told me about the audience reaction to his line 'I was adored once too' [II iii 174]. If he and Sir Toby were on good form, he said, it usually got *two* laughs. There was an immediate one, a response to the 'running gag' of Andrew's eagerness to agree with everything said by Sir Toby. But if the actors held the subsequent pause long enough the audience would laugh again, more quietly. This time their laughter contained a recognition of the pathos of the situation: how sad to have been adored only *once*; perhaps he's making even *that* up; perhaps he *knows* that he's making it up. But everything depended on the timing. When the second laugh didn't come, the actor said, he sometimes tried to force it by giving a sigh. 'And that *never* worked; it killed the laugh.'

This seems to me a good example of the precarious relationship between performance and text. Sir Andrew's line is perfectly intelligible, and thus does not get a footnote in the *Variorum*, Arden or Penguin editions of the play (though the Penguin editor's addition of a comma before 'too' is an implicit direction for speaking it). It can easily be passed over in reading. Yet it is likely to be an unforgettable moment in any good performance of *Twelfth Night*. Its blend of comedy and pathos, however, depends on the timing of the actors, the way in which Sir Toby looks at Sir Andrew before he speaks his next line, and factors beyond their control like whether someone coughs at the wrong moment. In production, then, the text can be made richer than the reader ever thought – or it can go for nothing.

No one can write much about *Twelfth Night* without stressing the complexity of feeling inherent in its plot – love is both sweet and painful, most jokes contain an element of cruelty, one person's success is another person's failure – and in the poetry and music which make up its atmosphere. Most directors recognise the need to do justice to this complexity, but, from the original casting to the final rehearsal, every choice that is made is going to tip the balance. As Ralph Berry puts it, in *Changing Styles in Shakespeare* (1981), 'The point lies in the constellation of relationships, in the overall system of checks and balances' (p. 113).

## 7   THE SETTING

One of the most important ways in which effects of balance and unity can be achieved is through the director's control of the visual impact of the play. The idea that each production should have its own set and costumes is a comparatively modern one, probably related to our belief in the importance of environmental influence on character. No setting can be completely neutral: a bare stage makes as much of a statement about the director's view of the play as one which represents a fishing village on an island off the coast of Dalmatia (Old Vic, 1950), the Balkans in the age of Byron (Prospect Touring Production, 1967), or a Berlin nightclub in the 1920s (Phoenix, Leicester, 1981). A pretty, highly stylised setting implies that we are to be ready for improbabilities of plot and emotion; a production full of realistic detail asks for a corresponding reality of feeling. But the two are not incompatible. In the 1955 Russian film, directed by Yan Fried, the peacocks strutting across the courtyard of Olivia's realistic palace were not only delightful to look at, they also symbolised the self-love and self-display in the play.

Costume can also be used to make characters seem more, or less, real. There are, of course, some suggestions about it in the text. Viola explains the fact that she and Sebastian are identically 'suited' by saying that she has imitated his style. In nineteenth-century productions, the sailors in I ii used to bring on a trunk, and lines were inserted for Viola to announce that she was going to wear the clothes contained in it; presumably Sebastian had two identical suits. (See the New Arden edition, 1975, edited by Lothian and Craik, p. lxxxii.) Olivia is certainly meant to be in mourning, and, strictly speaking, the rest of the household should follow her example, but in many productions only Malvolio does so. Directors who take an unsympathetic view of Olivia are likely to have her appear in a low-cut black dress, and to make her change from mourning attire to something incongruously bright for III i. What Maria wears will depend on the decision as to her social status. Scholars constantly insist that she should be a lady in waiting, but she is nearly always played as a chambermaid or housekeeper. When she tells the conspirators that Olivia 'abhors' the colour yellow, there is a traditional joke, most broadly played in the 1966 RSC production: 'everyone looked sorrowfully at Aguecheek, who at that moment realised that he had been fruitlessly wooing Olivia while dressed from head to foot in vilest yellow' (Hugh Leonard, *Plays and Players*, July 1966). Sometimes it is only a yellow scarf or ribbon that he wears.

It was characteristic of John Barton's RSC production to which I shall now turn, that his Sir Andrew was carrying a small bunch of yellow primroses, which he had been trying in vain to present to Olivia earlier in the play. At this point, he quietly and sadly got rid of them. This illustrates the way in which this production approached the characterisation of the comic figures. Of the four, it was much the most realistic in its use of detail to illuminate personal relationships, and in this respect it can be seen as a continuation of the style initiated in Peter Hall's famous 1958 *Twelfth Night*. Both productions, for instance, frequently showed characters eating and drinking and involved in mundane affairs: Hall's opened with Orsino having his portrait sketched, Barton's had courtiers bringing him papers to sign. Both dressed the characters in subdued colours which had an 'autumnal' effect and which also seemed more like real clothes than bright colours would have been. But Barton's production was part of a season which included the late romances of Shakespeare, and he was concerned to emphasise the affinity between *Twelfth Night* and the other plays which Northrop Frye has called 'tempest comedies' (*A Natural Perspective*, 1965, p. 137).

Thus, the basic setting was recognisably Jacobean, but it had been transformed:

> Upon a memory of rush-strewn floors and rush-lit galleries, Christopher Morley's designs fantasticate a skeletal Riviera of sun-streaked reed lattices, wicker garden furniture and parasols. By its half-lights and shades, a lotus-eating Duke and Countess embroider loving daydreams into which break the fleshly twins from the sea, Sebastian and Viola.
>
> (Ronald Bryden, *Observer*, 24 Aug. 1969)

It will be clear that we are here dealing with an interpretation of an interpretation. The set was also described as 'a long receding wattle tunnel' (J. W. Lambert, *The Sunday Times*, 24 Aug.) and as 'a kind of timeless Japanese tea-house' (Gordon

Parsons, *Morning Star*, 23 Aug.). Most spectators probably were
only vaguely aware of anything beyond the pleasing stage
pictures created by the light, which always seemed to be
coming from outside the set. One reviewer, on the other hand,
responded very fully:

> Outside we are aware of the bright day; inside the light is the muted
> gold of a winter garden, or the flickering yellow of a great candlelit
> hall. Outside, too, and throughout the play, the sea still tosses its
> waves: there are moments when the setting reminded me of the
> tunnel of a dream, a journeying place of the mind.
>                    (Sheila Bannock, *Stratford upon Avon Herald*, 29 Aug. 1969)

Everyone noticed the effective use which was made of the sound
of the sea, like the 'eternal note of sadness' of Arnold's 'Dover
Beach', beating against the enclosed world of human affections.
It was heard during Orsino's first speech, where it reinforced
his image of the 'spirit of love' receiving 'as the sea', and Viola
made her first long entrance from the back, through sea-smoke.
The sound and smoke recurred during Viola's conversation
with Orsino in II iv, and during her reunion with Sebastian.

Other offstage sounds, such as bird-song and the striking of
clocks, filled out the sense of a real world and emphasised the
passing of time. The sundial in Olivia's garden provided one of
the funniest moments in the play. In III iv, at the height of his
hubristic self-satisfaction, Malvolio compared his watch with it
– and corrected the *sundial*. What was so satisfying about this
piece of business was that it seemed psychologically true to the
character's egotism, while at the same time it was fully
integrated with the tone of the play. Malvolio is one of several
characters who try to do impossible things with time.

Music was also used extensively. Orsino was onstage
listening to a lutenist for a good fifteen minutes before the play
began. Everyone in the cast seemed to be humming Feste's
songs at odd moments (Jeremy Kingston, *Punch*, 3 Sept. 1969),
and Feste often underlined the mood of a scene by a phrase
from one of them. Viola whistled while he played his lute in
their little scene in III i. By making Sir Andrew a Scotsman with

1. *John Barton's RSC production, 1969.* The kitchen scene (Act II, scene iii): with Brenda Bruce as Maria, Emrys James as Feste, Barrie Ingham as Sir Andrew, Donald Sinden as Malvolio. Photo: Holte Photographics.

2. *Peter Gill's RSC production, 1974.* The kitchen scene: Frank Thornton as Sir Andrew, Ron Pember as Feste and David Waller as Sir Toby. Photo: Holte Photographics.

3. *Robin Midgley's production at the Haymarket Theatre, Leicester in 1979.* Pippa Guard as Viola and Malcolm Sinclair as Orsino. Photo: Jan Siegieda.

4. *Julian Lopez-Morillas's production at the Berkeley Shakespeare Festival, 1981.* Joan Mankin as Viola and Kevin Gardiner as Orsino. Photo: Alfred Bernard Stern.

5. *John Barton's RSC production, 1969*. Lisa Harrow as Olivia and Judi Dench as Viola. Photo: Holte Photographics.

6. *Julian Lopez-Morillas's production at the Berkeley Shakespeare Festival, 1981*. The 'Sir Topas' scene. Paul O'Connor as Malvolio in prison. Drew Lubarsky as Feste, impersonating Sir Topas, Robert Sinclair as Sir Toby, Marilyn Prince as Maria. Photo: Alfred Bernard Stern.

a set of bagpipes, Barton added a new 'running gag' to a character who seems fair game for any number of them (the climax came, inevitably, when Sir Toby sat on the pipes in III ii). He also extended the play's range of musical effects, particularly in the drinking scene. The main effect was melancholy; the phrase most often played and hummed was 'Youth's a stuff will not endure'.

Though Peter Gill's 1974 production was in Elizabethan costume, its context was not historical but literary: the world of Shakespeare's sonnets, which the actors studied, along with the play, during rehearsals. The set was dominated by a painted panel showing Narcissus gazing into a pool. On the walls were written two lines from the Sonnets: 'O learn to read what silent love hath writ' (no. 23) and 'O, know, sweet love, I always write of you' (no. 76). They seemed to point outward from the play, rather like programme notes, offering a biographical interpretation.

There was no attempt at recreating an Elizabethan social hierarchy. The reviewer in *The Times Educational Supplement* pointed out that Maria ought not to have sat down at her mistress's table without being asked, and that 'a Duke, even in Shakespeare's Illyria, looks odd if he hardly ever wears shoes' (John Peter, 24 Jan. 1975). Olivia, anachronistically, drank tea. Orsino's palace consisted of a bright-coloured carpet and large cushions on which he and his youthful court threw themselves. The Narcissus panel was moved around from time to time. Orsino made his first entrance from behind it, and one reviewer thought he could see 'a distinction between those characters who habitually turned themselves upstage and those – most notably Jane Lapotaire's Viola – who boldly addressed the audience, seeking a sounding-board rather than a mirror' (R. Cushman, *Observer*, 9 Feb. 1975). Another (Peter Thomson, *Shakespeare Survey 28*, 1975) noted the effect of the long Elizabethan-style entrances – especially Malvolio's – from two doors at the back of the stage. Other pieces of the set moved on and off as needed: a small enclosed chamber for the drinking scene, a tea table for Olivia, and various shrubs and trees in pots. The characters themselves sometimes took note, bemusedly, of these metamorphoses. The implication was that Illyria was a state of mind rather than a real place.

Robin Midgley set his *Twelfth Night* in Spain, because he wanted an atmosphere that would be both passionate and formal, one in which Malvolio's puritanism and his yellow-stockinged extravagance would be obvious deviations from a norm. The costumes were based mainly on Goya, with touches of Velasquez: Orsino was a Renaissance prince, but Viola and Sebastian were dressed, very becomingly, like Figaro in *The Barber of Seville*, and Olivia's veil was a mantilla. The sets and lighting evoked strong contrasts: outside were white walls and blazing sunshine; when the action moved to Olivia's house, trellises were dropped within the walls and the lighting changed to suggest a cool, shady interior.

Midgley followed the nineteenth-century practice of transposing the first two scenes. The play began in a limbo of blackness, after the storm, and then moved to the exterior of Olivia's house, where Orsino was pacing up and down, in blazing sunlight, awaiting the return of his messenger. By contrast, Olivia was then seen walking decorously in the confined space of her house, surrounded by black-dressed members of the older generation: the priest, Feste, Malvolio. Even Orsino's servant Valentine was played as a stiff, elderly man, dressed like Malvolio. He was the 'nuncio of more grave aspect' [I iv 28] with whom Orsino contrasts the young Cesario. Visually, everything was prepared for the effect of the page's first entrance, when youth and life would seem to burst in upon the cloistered Olivia. It was this contrast which the production was primarily concerned to show.

The Berkeley production was put on during the Christmas season (2 December 1981–10 January 1982), and was given a context of mid-winter revels: the programme notes discussed Renaissance music and the custom of a Feast of Misrule. The audience was invited to enter into this spirit by coming early to buy food and drink, which could be taken into the auditorium, and to listen to a pre-play concert.

The hall was festooned with greenery, branches of holly and

(electric) candles. The set was an unlocalised platform with a mezzanine gallery for the musicians; the few essential properties were stored beneath it, and it also served as the dark house for Malvolio. The stage made no pretence of being anything but a space for acting and singing, and there was very little naturalistic business. Characters frequently entered from the audience. Costumes were inspired by the look of Merrie England as seen on a Christmas card. Sir Toby's orange and red colouring was obviously meant to associate him with the Lord of Misrule, and his cohorts wore somewhat paler shades of the same colours. Outsiders – Viola, Sebastian, Antonio and the sailors – wore sober blue and black. Only Malvolio and Olivia were dressed in black at the beginning; Orsino, interestingly, was in black and red; Olivia moved gradually out of mourning, first by adding white sleeves to her black dress and later by changing into red, thus aligning herself with the forces of Yule.

The most important feature of the production was the constant presence of the musicians. During the last half hour before it started, they performed folk songs, many of which were bawdy and rumbustious. The more serious items were introduced near the end as various characters, including Orsino, wandered down the aisles to listen. After that, the musicians withdrew to the gallery where they were always ready to accompany Feste's songs or furnish actors for the smaller parts. The musical element in the play was greatly expanded: thus, Viola's first entry was preceded by a sea shanty, and sailors ran down the aisles hauling imaginary ropes while she dragged herself up to the platform. At the start of I iii, Malvolio and Olivia, in black, entered at one side, watched by the brightly dressed Toby and Maria at the other, and listened respectfully to a song of mourning. When Antonio and Sebastian arrived in Illyria they were surrounded by musical street cries which inspired Antonio's suggestion that Sebastian might need his purse. Malvolio's exit to go and put on his yellow stockings, which concluded the first half of the play, led into a rendition of 'Give me my yellow hose again' by the musicians, who moved back to stage centre. Thus, everything, including Malvolio's deception, was located in the context of revelry. Sir Toby's 'Dost thou think, because thou art virtuous, there shall be no more cakes and ale?' [II iii 111–12] was played straight at the audience (many of whom had pints of ale in their hands) and accompanied by murmurs of assent from the musicians. There could be no doubt where sympathy was meant to lie.

All four productions were pleasing to look at and did full justice to the music; *Twelfth Night* is a play which seems to require visual and aural beauty. The musical elaboration which added to the melancholy of the 1969 RSC version served equally well, in the Berkeley version, to create a sense of festive jollity. Visually, each production created its own sense of the patterns within the play. Barton and Gill used the set and costumes to suggest a basic similarity between the 'romantic' and 'comic' characters, with only Malvolio standing apart in his grotesque costume and make-up. Midgley and Lopez-Morillas, on the other hand, emphasised the contrasts between characters: heat versus cold, youth versus age, in the first; Carnival versus Lent in the second . All these interpretations can be justified from the text, which contains both harmony and discord. The test of their effectiveness must be how well they were able to fulfil its romantic and comic demands.

## 8   ROMANCE

> Jove knows I love;
>     But who?
> Lips, do not move;
>     No man must know.

[II v 95–8]

That Olivia might be suffering from a violent, concealed passion for Malvolio is hardly less likely than some of the things that actually do happen in *Twelfth Night*. Sudden emotional reactions are the object of mockery in *As You Like It*; here, they are taken for granted. Their language is understatement. Olivia has to convey the awakening of her love for Cesario in the line 'You might do much. / What is your parentage?' [I v 265–6]. Viola's grief at her brother's loss is conveyed so briefly that Felicity Kendal, who played the part in the BBC TV production, found her first scene 'the most difficult in my life. Viola's life is shattered, yet it is written very simply – it can seem rather glib' (the BBC TV Shakespeare edition, 1979, p. 25).

That the actors were expected to convey emotion through means other than speech is clear from Viola's comment on Olivia's behaviour:

> She made good view of me, indeed so much
> That – methought – her eyes had lost her tongue,
> For she did speak in starts, distractedly.
>
> [II ii 19–21]

If the sense of 'glibness' is to be avoided, the words of this subdued and secret love must be surrounded by an aura of feeling. It is this aspect of a production that is hardest to convey. Comic stage business can be documented and described but it is difficult to show exactly *how* the nature of Viola's love for Orsino emerges in the tone of her voice when she calls him 'my lord' or in the way she looks at him as they both sit listening to Feste's song.

The play thus seems to invite a style of production which goes between the lines in search of the subtext. The problem is to know the point at which playing between the lines becomes playing *against* the lines. This is particularly important in the treatment of Olivia and Orsino. Because both characters change their minds in the course of the play, it has become a critical cliché to contrast them unfavourably with Viola – as when Hugh Hunt and Peter Hall write that Orsino is in love with love, Olivia is in love with grief, and only Viola represents sincere love (see Hunt, *Old Vic Prefaces*, 1966, p. 57, and Hall's preface to Folio Society edition, p. 3). Hunt's argument was that a satirical portrayal of Orsino and Olivia made for a better

balance between the comic and romantic interests of the play,
and this was also borne out in Hall's 1958 production, where
Geraldine McEwan's Olivia turned out to be the funniest and
most memorable of the performances. The difficulty with this
view is that it devalues the language which Orsino and Olivia
speak. To encourage the audience to laugh at a man who says
'If music be the food of love, play on' can look like a tacit
agreement between director and audience that poetry is really
pretty silly stuff. To emphasise Orsino's egotism or silliness is
also to shift the emphasis of Viola's role. Playing both Orsino
and Olivia as very young is one way of allowing them to be silly
without losing the audience's sympathy. All four of the
productions discussed here had a young Olivia; their concepts
of Orsino were more varied.

John Barton's production was particularly remembered for
its 'glimpses of unspoken tenderness' (Bryden, *Observer*, 24
Aug. 1969), or 'unspoken communion' (Irving Wardle, *The
Times*, 22 Aug. 1969). This obviously implies a strong emphasis
on the subtext. The director assumed that *everyone's* feelings
mattered: Sir Andrew's pathetic courtship of Olivia, Maria's
relationship with Sir Toby, and, above all, Viola and Orsino.
The key to all these relationships was the pervading melancholy of the interpretation. Bryden felt that Richard Pasco's
Orsino had 'a passion which goes beyond love. He feeds his
desire on the thought of mortality. Before the dark oblivion
which fills his mind with the sound of waves crashing on
Illyria's shore, he will have someone to lighten his loneliness'
(*Observer*, 9 Aug. 1970). Our sense of Orsino comes very much
from the way in which the other characters treat him. Here, the
only point at which he seemed to be mocked was in Feste's
singing of 'Come Away Death', for which the Fool adopted an
exaggeratedly tragic manner as if to show Orsino how excessive
his melancholy looked from the outside. Only Viola, of course,
recognised what was going on. But in the conversation which
followed, one felt not only the genuineness of Viola's love but
also that of her master's death-wish. When he asked, 'But *died*
thy sister of her love, my boy?', the question not only recalled
the song to which they had been listening, it also showed his

awareness of the destructive nature of his passion for Olivia. That these two characters should both be acquainted with grief made a bond between them. Lisa Harrow's Olivia, despite her sophistication and wit, seemed much younger. Bryden felt that she was attracted to the disguised Viola because this figure had 'none of the adult danger and urgency of sex' (*Observer*, 9 Aug. 1970).

Judi Dench's Viola was an extremely varied performance. Though she was particularly remembered for her sensitivity to the poetry and romance of the part, she also brought out other aspects of it. In I ii, she was affectionately demonstrative to the sailors, and, in the scene before the mock-duel, she surprised Fabian with an equally affectionate embrace when he offered to placate her adversary. Her conversation with Feste in III i, broken by an interval while he played his lute and she whistled, suggested to Wardle that they were both 'ruefully surveying the human scene from some other plane' (*The Times*, 22 Aug. 1969). When Malvolio came panting after her in II ii (here played before II i), she displayed mock-solicitude, helping him to a bench and slapping him on the back. At the same time, through careful timing and use of pauses, she was able to suggest layers of emotional reality behind her words. Some reviewers found the pauses excessive. B. A. Young transcribed her first line as 'What country: friends. Is this' (*Financial Times*, 22 Aug. 1969). The slow pace was, however, perfectly suited to the scene with Orsino in II iv, with all its sadly ironic double meanings. Jeremy Kingston's description of her 'following a catch in her voice with a light laugh' (*Punch*, 3 Sept. 1969) shows how she embodied the 'smiling at grief' which Viola describes in her most famous speech.

Maria's love for Sir Toby seemed to parallel Viola's for Orsino, in that it was silent and, much of the time, seemed hopeless. In fact, the production *created* this relationship by redistributing entrances and exits, and redirecting lines, to an extent which fell just short of rewriting. Instead of being the small, pert figure implied by the jokes in the text, Maria was played as middle-aged and maternally solicitous for the drunken Toby, who often treated her badly. Stanley Wells, in

*Royal Shakespeare* (1976), traces the ways in which this relationship was developed in the production. It culminated in Sir
Toby's slipping a ring on Maria's finger when he said 'Come by
and by to my chamber', while Feste underlined the mood of the
scene by strumming 'Youth's a stuff will not endure' in the
background. She was, naturally, on stage in the last scene as
well, and Wardle remembered her 'glare of possessive indignation' at Sebastian 'for having clobbered her hero' (*The Times*, 7
Aug. 1970). (All directors except Lopez-Morillas, incidentally,
brought Maria onstage for the final scene, despite the absence
of any reference to her in the text of the play.) If she were played
as the waiting gentlewoman that scholars insist she is, then the
almost unprepared announcement of her marriage to Sir Toby
would seem no odder than Gratiano's abrupt announcement in
*The Merchant of Venice* that he has been courting Nerissa while
Bassanio courted Portia [III ii 190–213]. But a director who
decides to stress the disparity between her and Toby has to
provide them with a greater sense of context. At the RST in 1979,
Terry Hands found a further level of bitterness in the relationship by having Toby and Maria remain on stage to the end of
Act V; they were thus able to hear the derisive laughter with
which the other characters greeted the news of their marriage.
Barton was kinder to them, and indeed to all the characters. He
did not necessarily make them all happy at the end, but he took
them seriously as people, and had them take each other
seriously as well.

Barton's production is still something of a legend, and it may
be some time before anyone else goes as far in that particular
mode of psychological subtlety and romantic atmosphere. Yet
it was the culmination of a naturalistic school of drama (also
represented by Hall's production of 1958/60), rather than a
specifically twentieth-century interpretation. (It is significant,
for instance, that both Hall and Barton were often compared to
Chekhov.)

The RSC production which followed Barton's, that of Peter
Gill in 1974, drew on contemporary interest in sexual experi-
ment, which could be compared to the Renaissance interest in
androgyny and the custom of boy actors. Clifford Leech writes,

of the scenes between Olivia and Viola, 'More than usually in Shakespeare we are made conscious of the sex of the players, the sex of the characters they are playing, and the double disguise of the boy playing Viola' (*'Twelfth Night' and Shakespearean Comedy*, p. 49). Diana Rigg, who had played Viola at the RST in 1966, commented in an interview on this aspect of the play:

> It was bound to have been even funnier originally, the complexity of the situation between Olivia and Viola: a boy-playing-a-girl who falls in love with a boy-playing-a-girl-playing-a-boy. . . . But I think the really clever thing that Shakespeare posed – and this is something that is not done by contemporary playwrights – is a sexuality which is not based on the extremes of feminism or masculinism that we have nowadays.
>
> (*Plays and Players*, June 1973)

It was this kind of sexuality that Gill's production sought to explore.

The atmosphere was highly charged with erotic feeling, yet the tone of Orsino's court was surprisingly casual, perhaps because of the youth of the characters. The young men took physical contact for granted; Orsino had his arm around Curio in the first scene. They were always shadow-boxing, tumbling about on the cushions, then darting off 'like puppies on a sunlit lawn' (J. W. Lambert, *The Sunday Times*, 25 Aug. 1974). Viola was shadow-boxing with Valentine at the start of I iv, and when Orsino addressed her she showed that she was expecting more of the same. Instead, as he urged her to go to Olivia's house on his behalf, he pinned her arms behind her back and, as he declared that 'all is semblative a woman's part', he ran his hand down her body. It was hard to know whether Gill meant to emphasise Orsino's blindness, to tease the audience ('Does he know or doesn't he?'), or to depict Illyria as a Garden of Eden in which sexual desire was not recognised for what it was. Antonio and Sebastian were equally demonstrative and were seen embracing in both their scenes; even Olivia was given to touching people: she poked both Feste and Malvolio with her fan in her first scene and her behaviour towards the steward was sufficiently provocative to explain his belief that she was in love with him. Even at the end, as she explained the deceit that had been practised on him, she laid her hand on his shoulder. In the scenes between Viola and Olivia, reviewers were not sure whether it was the supposed boy or the real girl that Olivia was fondling. Violence was also expressed physically: Antonio reacted to Sebastian's supposed perfidy by grabbing Viola by the throat and then pushing her away; Orsino seized both Olivia and Viola in the final scene, and on 'Farewell', pushed Viola violently toward her supposed wife.

One reviewer felt that Jane Lapotaire's Viola seemed 'guilt-ridden' (Michael Billington, *Guardian*, 6 Feb. 1975), but most commented simply on her vitality and the ease with which she carried off her master–mistress role. Even on her first entry she hardly seemed forlorn; as B. A. Young notes, her 'breathless trotting' round the stage conveyed no sense of shipwreck or destitution (*Financial Times*, 23 Aug. 1974), and by the end of the scene she was already pinning up her hair, ready for her new role.

The emphasis of the production was erotic rather than emotional. Where Barton used pauses, Gill used physical contact to point up the developing relationships. A good example is his treatment of II iv. As it began, Orsino was reclining on his cushions, with his court, listening to the music; Viola sat between his knees. 'How dost thou like this tune?', her reply, and his 'Thou dost speak masterly' were pitched at the same languorous level. Then, a thought striking him, he sat up and asked if the boy had ever been in love. The next bit of dialogue was taken very lightly, as they rolled about together on the cushions – Orsino laughing at the idea of Cesario's older, masculine-looking mistress, Viola both delighted and terrified. At Feste's entrance the court settled itself again, and everyone leaned back to listen to the song, but Viola and Orsino, now holding hands, gradually sat up. For her speech about her 'sister', she was sitting and he kneeling beside her. At 'But died thy sister . . .?' he turned her face towards his.

The production succeeded almost too well in being ambiguous. Most reviewers assumed that Orsino was meant to be bisexual, and one suggested that the main influence was Oscar Wilde (Victoria Radin, *Observer*, 25 Aug. 1974). J. W. Lambert, however, saw in the young lovers 'that element of comradeship or soul friendship, going in no terror of physical contact, which is merely demeaned by bleakly oversimplifying words like bisexuality' (*The Sunday Times*, 25 Aug. 1974). The sense of ambiguity was kept up to the end. Sebastian's entrance – with a special light on him, after the two knights had left the stage – was almost magical. Yet Olivia's reaction was comical. Wardle describes her 'licking her lips at the sight of the interchangeably delicious twins' (*The Times*, 6 Feb. 1975), and her 'Most wonderful!' brought the house down. On 'Cesario, come!' Orsino caught at the wrong twin. Olivia, as she moved away with Sebastian, looked back half wistfully at Viola, perhaps wishing that it were after all possible to have both.

It has become customary in modern productions to emphasise the isolation of Antonio, like his counterpart in *The Merchant of Venice*, from final happiness. In Barton's production, he went off in a different direction from the two couples at the end. In the context of a frankly erotic world like that of Gill's production, his reactions were a particularly important part of the final scene. During Viola's brief account of herself to Sebastian (she took off her sword and handed it to Curio), Antonio turned to look out front. The implication, I think, was that he had just tasted the fruit of the Tree of Knowledge: he realised, that is, the nature and the hopelessness of his feelings for Sebastian. The play ended with a dance into which the lovers drew him for a while; then they went out behind the Narcissus panel; it closed behind them, and Antonio was left staring at it as Feste sang the closing song. This was the most insistent treatment of the homosexual possibilities inherent in the Renaissance ideal of friendship. Like Irving's Malvolio, it brings out something which is potentially rather than actually present in the text.

Midgley's production was less obviously experimental, but its stress on the contrast between passion and repression was post-Freudian, even Lawrentian, and the Spanish setting helped to free the actors from Anglo-Saxon restraint. The transposition of the first two scenes meant that the play began with the fairytale situation of the heroine arriving, in tatters, on an unknown coast. Only after this frail and helpless-looking girl had decided to take service with the Duke did the audience get their first glimpse of him: what Midgley wanted was the sense of a savage animal and of the danger that Viola was entering into. While the Byronic quality of self-awareness in Malcolm Sinclair's brooding Orsino somewhat undercut this directorial interpretation, he nevertheless came closer than any other Orsino in my experience to the figure described by Wilson Knight (who had played the part himself): 'He should not be presented as a sentimental young man, but rather as a barbaric prince, somewhat oriental, of a passionate and violent nature. His name is significant' (*Shakespearean Production*, 1964, p. 83). Orsino means bear; Sinclair was hardly that, but he was able to bring off the homicidal outburst of the final scene without incongruity.

Pippa Guard's Viola approached this dangerous character with the coolness of one who was used to taking risks and, in her scenes with him, preserved a sense of apartness and secretiveness which was itself attractive. With Olivia, she was quite unsentimental. The relationship between these two women was one which both actresses found extremely interesting. Viola was harsh to Olivia not so much because of her treatment of Orsino as because, being a woman herself, she knew what it meant for another woman to choose to shut herself away from the light. The blonde young Olivia (Joanne Pearce) looked strange in her black clothes, surrounded by elderly figures in black. Her bursting into life under the influence of Cesario's presence was both funny and frightening: Midgley's image for it was of a plant suddenly being moved from darkness into the sun. The bright sunlight of the final scene seemed to bathe all the characters in its beneficent warmth; only Malvolio came from, and returned to, the darkness.

The comedy-orientated Berkeley production seemed at first to be taking a rather perfunctory view of the romantic characters. Its Orsino came nearer to caricature than any of the others.

He and his household were given to a solemn, 'romantic' style, which might be natural for him but was artificial for them. In the first scene Curio and Valentine could be seen anxiously glancing at each other behind his back – not so much ridiculing their master as wondering what he would do next. His behaviour in the first part of II iv was played for laughs. After 'come, the song we had last night', Feste signalled to the musicians to begin. Orsino went on 'Mark it Cesario', and proceeded to talk through the music. Feste waved the musicians to stop. Orsino again indicated that he should begin, again found himself irresistibly impelled to add a few more programme notes. Again, Feste stopped the introduction. Politely but drily, he enquired 'Are you ready, sir?' After the song, he pretended to refuse Orsino's tip, with an exaggeratedly soulful 'No pains, sir. I take pleasure in singing, sir', which was recognisably a parody of the grand style of the Orsino household.

The most interesting aspect of the production was its treatment of Viola. Only a *comic* heroine could fall in love with a self-dramatising Orsino, and this Viola was essentially comic, with the wry, self-deprecating humour often found in American women comedians. She was *not* the touchstone by which the sincerity of the other characters was to be measured. Her first scene showed her completely helpless, longing to give up, or to find someone else to look after her. The news that Olivia had just lost a brother too made her cry out with grief. In men's clothes, she was uncomfortable, found her sword awkward, and kept trying to pull her tunic down. She 'caught' love from Orsino as one might catch a disease, and Olivia caught the 'plague' from her. At times it seemed as if the production had blended the obvious convention of the Feast of Misrule with another convention, that of the Hollywood romantic comedy, where the faithful down-trodden secretary adores her boss from afar. But the actress (Joan Mankin, who was also artistic director of a feminist theatre group) gave hints of something more interesting. For instance, when Viola is used as a mouthpiece for a conventional generalisation about the weaknesses of women –

How easy is it for the proper false
In women's waxen hearts to set their forms.
Alas, our fraility is the cause, not we;
For such as we are made, if such we be.           [II ii 29–32]

– the actress, forgetting her doublet and hose, dropped a
mock-curtsey which was also a mock-acknowledgement of the
sexual stereotyping in the lines.

Paradoxically, the very absence of romantic idealisation of
Viola was what suggested the presence of a feminist perspective
in this production. She was a human being, not an embodiment
of a dream of perfect, self-sacrificing love. It is arguable that
both the plot and the poetry of the play work against any real
attempt to import a feminist reading: Shakespeare's heroines
tend to be idealised precisely in proportion to their passivity,
and Viola's powerlessness to affect the action has often been
noticed. The Berkeley production relied on conventional
responses to carry off the final couplings. It was characteristic
that the other characters should react with pleasure at the news
of Sir Toby's marriage to Maria, whom he carried on at the
curtain call. The other marriages were accepted, not because
they were psychologically probable, but because the production had established an atmosphere in which marriage was
obviously a Good Thing. This frank acceptance of improbabil-
ity did not seem to me out of keeping with the spirit of the play.


## 9   COMEDY


One can sympathise to some extent with the eighteenth-
century annotator of *Bell's Edition of Shakespeare*, who wrote of
some of the repartee in II iii: 'There is very little doubt but
*Shakespeare* had some meaning, in this scene; however to us it
plainly appears, that he took uncommon pains to conceal the
greatest part of it.' The obscurity of the verbal jokes was
probably one reason why Feste's role was of comparatively

little importance in the eighteenth century, whereas Malvolio's, which depends much more on situation than on language, dominated the play. Nowadays, one can read the play in heavily annotated editions which explain all but a few of the jokes, but the director still has to decide what to do with them in performance. This decision will have an important effect on the tone of the play. If Feste's jokes cannot be made funny, he must be interpreted as an unsuccessful, or unhappy, clown – or as something totally different.

Thus, some productions elevate Feste to an almost superhuman position. Reviewers of both RSC productions thought that the play was being seen through his eyes. He knew instinctively that Cesario was Viola, for instance. More recently, he has been a sort of stage-manager: at Ashland, Oregon, in 1974, he controlled the lighting with magic gestures; at the RST in 1979 he was onstage throughout, pottering about with bits of scenery and cueing the characters' entrances. Sometimes there are hints of absurdist theatre in his portrayal, sometimes a touch of anarchy, as in other famous clowns. This interpretation seems to have got out of hand when one Feste can be described as 'far more of a killjoy than Malvolio' (Hugh Leonard, *Plays and Players*, July 1972) and another as being 'perversely determined never to get any laughs from his material' (Geoff Brown, *Plays and Players*, May 1977).

Ron Pember's Feste, in the Peter Gill production, made some spectators uncomfortable; as one reviewer put it, he 'mutters at Olivia, growls at Viola, rages at Orsino, sneers at Malvolio, and then turns on the audience with such savagery that the closing line "we strive to please you every day", comes across as a promise to flay us en masse in the foyer' (Benedict Nightingale, *New Statesman*, 14 Feb. 1975). I quote this because it seems to represent the view of more than one critic, but my own recollection is of a hard-bitten Cockney professional, without illusions but not without feelings. He could sing both high- and low-brow, depending on the taste of his audience, but preferred the latter. His repertoire included some mild conjuring tricks, such as making the coins he begged disappear up his sleeve.

Roy Macready's Feste, at Leicester in 1979, was also conceived as a competent professional, but he was elderly and bespectacled, and clearly belonged to the world of Olivia's father rather than to the newer generation. His jokes and music were good enough, but everyone had heard them before. Midgley took the view that Malvolio, although a humourless critic, was not far wrong in his derogatory remarks in I v. But the character was still allowed to get laughs, and some of the unintelligible double-talk [II iii] was made funny by the use of a banner (inspired by a Goya painting) in the shape of a grotesque head, through whose mouth he put his fingers to make it 'talk'.

The portrayal of Feste illustrates most sharply the problem of dealing with the comic business in *Twelfth Night*. In even the most sober production, it is likely that the spectator who knows the play only from reading will be surprised at how much visual humour it contains. This falls into two categories, which may be defined as explanatory and decorative. The former is used in order to bring out the meaning of the lines. In the case of bawdy jokes and double-entendres, like the pun on C, U, T and P when Malvolio is reading Maria's forged letter, reactions – bewilderment on Sir Andrew's part, an aghast double-take on Malvolio's – may be enough to make clear the nature, if not the exact meaning, of what has been said. A traditional bawdy piece of business is for Maria, when she says, 'bring your hand to the buttery bar and let it drink' [I iii 66–7], to place Sir Andrew's hand on her breast. This is probably what the original boy-actor did – though then, of course, it would have been a different kind of joke. Leslie Hotson has found (in *The First Night of 'Twelfth Night'*) more bawdy jokes than anyone had previously suspected in the Fool's role; though not all his suggestions have been widely accepted, it is useful to remember that fools were on the whole associated with a crude kind of humour, as suggested by the phallic bawble they carried.

The decorative type of stage business is likely to be more controversial. Academic reviewers constantly accuse directors of playing *Twelfth Night* too farcically. Yet most of its comic scenes rely on established farce devices – drunkenness, eavesdropping, a mock mad scene and a mock duel. Is it possible to fix a point beyond which comic business should not be allowed to go? It may help to look at a few of the scenes for which it is most important.

Perhaps because some of the lines in II iii are so difficult to understand, this scene has a long tradition of comic business, much of it depending on the obvious joke of watching Sir Toby and Sir Andrew getting increasingly drunk and incapable. In the eighteenth and nineteenth centuries (see A. C. Sprague, *Shakespeare and the Actors*, 1944, pp. 6–7), they would try vainly to light their pipes from a candle, fall over, and pull each other onto the floor, so that 'Sir Toby, there you lie' [II iii 104] became a visual pun. Malvolio's entrance has become more and more ludicrous over the years. Some directors have taken the view, not unreasonably, that such a character would hardly be likely to try to enforce his authority without first getting properly dressed, but from at least the time of Irving (1884) he has worn a dressing gown and nightcap. This nightcap is likely to be snatched from his head by the revellers in the confrontation which follows, and they may also trip him up, try to look up his nightshirt, and so on.

There are two objections to overdoing the easy comic effects here. One is that a Malvolio who looks too ridiculous may anticipate the more startling metamorphosis which Shakespeare devised for him. Yellow stockings can seem almost an anticlimax after some of the ways in which Malvolio has been dressed: with curlers in his hair and even (when Beerbohm-Tree played him in 1901) on his moustache; in a hairnet; with a Teddy bear under his gown (at Stratford, Ontario, in 1980).

Another danger of the over-farcical approach is pointed out in Alan Brien's review of the RSC's 1966 *Twelfth Night*, which was particularly full of comic stage-business:

> David Warner as Sir Andrew waltzes round behind a big oak settle with Maria in his arms and appears at the other side embracing Malvolio. . . . Mr. Warner's boozy, hesitant temerity, as he works up to snatching Malvolio's long white knitted nightcap, is admirably paced, and Ian Holm's horrid embarrassment when his nest of hair curlers is revealed provides an unexpected denoue-

ment. But, afterwards, Malvolio no longer seems a worthwhile victim of the hoaxes and the forged letter becomes a nasty and pointless joke.

(Sunday Telegraph, 19 June 1966)

In fact, as A. C. Sprague pointed out long ago, 'It is Malvolio who gives offence here; Malvolio who provokes vengeance' (*Shakespeare and the Actors*, p. 7). However funny the scene may be, its main point is that the steward has stopped everyone's fun and threatened to use his influence with Olivia against them. This was made extremely clear in the Barton production, where what Malvolio interrupted was a 'kind of mock-courtship of Maria' (Wells, *Royal Shakespeare*, p. 52) through music and dancing. The sung dialogue between Toby and Feste became a secret code in which they argued as to whether Toby could 'dare' to defy the steward. Maria's revenge on Malvolio was motivated both by the threat to her own position and by the danger to Sir Toby. The fact that, at this stage, Malvolio was really in command was made clear despite the absurd appearance of Donald Sinden's Malvolio, in a short nightshirt over which he wore the steward's chain (the implication was that he never took it off even in bed). As he told them off, he took their glasses from them, and on his last line he blew out the candles and went off with the tray of refreshments which they had brought in at the beginning. In the Midgley production, though the other characters made fun of Malvolio, he succeeded in spoiling their fun by removing, not the ale, but the cake: a large frosted one which Sir Andrew had been lovingly holding on his lap.

The other scene which demands extra comic business is the mock duel. It is particularly difficult to handle in that it requires the cooperation of comic and non-comic actors, whereas in the Malvolio scenes it is possible for the performers to compete without ever interacting. The comedy of Viola's part comes from the tremulous politeness which she maintains throughout ('Pray sir, put your sword up, if you please'), whereas almost anything goes where Sir Andrew is concerned. I have seen him draw his scabbard and throw away the sword, get his sword caught in the branches of a tree, and collapse during the duel under the mistaken impression that he had just been killed. The scene probably works best when most of the time is taken up with elaborate preparations (in Barton's production, Fabian rolled bandages while talking to Viola). Hall in 1958 had a great deal of saluting, flourishing, taking off of hats and so on (with Viola carefully copying Sir Andrew). A complicated bit of sword-exchanging among the participants probably derived from the hat-swopping in *Waiting for Godot* (1956), which in turn was based on a famous Marx Brothers routine. After they had used every possible delaying tactic, Viola and Sir Andrew finally took up positions, saluted again, and, with wonderful unanimity, ran off in opposite directions.

While one would readily agree that II iii should not be *only* a drunken scene, and III iv should not be *only* a series of jokes about comic cowardice, a production which fails to find laughs in either scene must surely have its emphasis wrong. While the Barton production was initially criticised for being too melancholy, it got funnier in successive revivals. The subtle interconnections between the other characters did not extend to Malvolio, who was thus able to play in a comic style which some reviewers recognised, rightly, as totally different from that of the rest of the production. Only in the 'dark house' scene, when he tried to persuade Feste to help him, was there a sense that he was trying for once, to speak as one human being to another. He was grotesque – Ronald Bryden was reminded of Humpty Dumpty, though Sinden himself said that he had modelled himself on a painting of Somerset Maugham – and there was no attempt to make him behave like a real-life steward, except that he occasionally banged his staff of office on the floor to make a point, for instance to silence Maria's laughter at one of Feste's jokes in I v. At the start of I iii he and Olivia were seen passing across the stage on the way, presumably, to prayers, and his presence in I v was so oppressive that he got one laugh on his first entrance and another on his first word, a grudging 'Ye-es' which seemed wrung from him by torture. His lack of the generosity which this play celebrates was also shown, as Gareth Lloyd Evans pointed out, in another inventive piece of business as he struggled to get the ring off his finger to give to Viola (*Shakespeare Survey 23*, 1970).

There was no suggestion that Malvolio actually *loved* Olivia – something which would of course make him pathetic – so the fiendish ingenuity of his deciphering of the letter and his knowing air when he next met Olivia could be enjoyed as a study in rampant egotism. The 'dark house' scene was played cruelly, however, with Feste dancing on the trap door above him and, at one point, slamming the lid down on his fingers. Maria, Toby and Feste themselves were aware of the cruelty and ashamed of it; Feste showed weary self-disgust as he removed his priest's disguise, and compassion as he agreed to bring pen and ink to the prisoner. In the final scene, Ronald Bryden remembered 'Olivia's troubled glance after Malvolio as the abused steward thrusts his chain of office into her hands and stumbles away' (*Observer*, 24 Aug. 1969). It seemed odd that such a towering figure should end up so completely broken, but the interpretation was in keeping with the tone of the final scene, where happiness was only muted. J. C. Trewin records a tradition, used by Donald Wolfit, in which 'the man – presumably entreated to a peace – would kneel before Olivia and in dumb-show receive his chain' (*Going to Shakespeare*, p. 167). Few directors nowadays are eager to end on a note of reconciliation. Malvolio is more likely to be the object of cruel laughter from the rest of the cast, as he walks into the scenery or is tripped up by his cross-gartering.

The main difficulty with the Peter Gill production, it was generally agreed, was that it worked much better for the serious characters than for the comic ones. The Narcissus idea was really relevant only for Malvolio, and, as Rosemary Say wrote, 'In such a performance there is little place for the comics, save as feed men to towering conceit' (*Sunday Telegraph*, 13 Jan. 1975). David Waller, who played Sir Toby, thought that the character's ostentatious jollity was a case of protesting too much; in an interview, he pointed out that Toby as well as Olivia had been bereaved: 'he's just lost a brother and a nephew' (*Guardian*, 18 Sept. 1974). Maria was brisk and harassed; after Feste's hint about her relationship with Toby, she emphasised her 'Peace, you rogue, no more o' that' by slapping his face. Sir Andrew's performance was remembered for the glum way in which he asked 'Shall we set about some revels?' Sir Toby and Fabian were grimly amused at their trick on him, and Fabian mimed a throat-cutting gesture as they discussed the forthcoming duel. Naturally, some reviewers wondered why such an uncheerful household should be so hostile to the anti-festive spirit as embodied in Malvolio.

There was so much critical disagreement about what Gill and Williamson were trying to do with the character of Malvolio that it is hard not to suspect that something went wrong somewhere with the interpretation. Some critics thought that he was meant to be a Scots elder, others took him for a Welsh Puritan. One reason for the confusion may have been that this repressed character was trying to repress his original accent as well; B. A. Young thought that it returned 'in full flood when the unhappy man is tied up in the cellar' (*Financial Times*, 23 Aug. 1974). Olivia's habit of touching him had obviously had its effect; even before he read the forged letter, 'his dreams of lust in the garden were terrible to overhear' (Robert Cushman, *Observer*, 9 Feb. 1975). He played the letter-reading scene seated, crossing and uncrossing his legs, and rising only to thank 'Jove'. The final instruction, that he should smile when in Olivia's presence, obviously has great comic potential if Malvolio has been grimly unsmiling up to this point. It provided the most memorable moment of Williamson's performance:

> A smile (his first?) suggests itself, spreading like cracks over paving stone, followed by a tentative, deep-throated but to him Dionysiac 'ho Ho!' We know that he is lost.
>
> (Peter Ansorge, *Plays and Players*, July 1974)

His encounter with Olivia demonstrated rampant lust – he stamped his feet impatiently during the servant's brief interruption – and after her departure he helped himself to a cup of tea from her table, then 'sprawled' beside it in 'gangling self-love' (Peter Thomson, *Shakespeare Survey*, 1975). His final moments showed the madness run full course, as he shielded his eyes from the sun and, presumably, from enlightenment.

The recent tendency to play the comic characters as elderly can have a sobering effect on their part of the play; 'Youth's a stuff will not endure' has a different meaning if sung to two elderly drunks by an elderly Fool. This was what happened in the Midgley *Twelfth Night*. Sir Toby, though able to totter about, spent much of his time in a wheelchair, pushed by Fabian. Midgley saw him as Sir Toby's batman, who had looked after him during his wilder years. Now the knight was having to resign himself to being an old man: the tricking of Malvolio was a final defiant gesture, and the disastrous confrontation with Sebastian marked the end of his self-delusion. One sign of his resignation was his marriage to Maria, a very motherly housekeeper who was first seen hanging out clothes to dry; she came on with him in the final scene and, taking over Fabian's nursemaid role, tucked a rug over his knees before wheeling him off.

This production was also notable for a baby-faced *fat* Sir Andrew; Midgley felt that Sir Toby's jokes about his appearance were meant to go by contraries. I remember his stricken look when Malvolio went off with the cake, and his dramatic miming of the challenge to Cesario, obviously the result of much labour, while Toby and Fabian unrolled the immensely long scroll on which he had written it. Malvolio was not really wrong in calling their behaviour uncivil. He himself, though stuffy, was not incredible or fantastic until after he had read the letter. It was clear from his expression that he did *not* remember Olivia commending his yellow stockings, but he conscientiously talked himself into the idea that she had. The production used familiar jokes, like having Malvolio inadvertently tie the two legs of his cross-garters together. But the funnier he became in his infatuation, the more disturbing the final effect was. In the final scene Midgley emphasised the extent of the steward's humiliation by having him enter at the same spot where he had appeared in full authority in I v and II iii. Now he was only in shirt and trousers, without even his steward's chain, covered in dust and blinded by the sun. His departure brought no laughter, and it took the others some time to pull themselves back to the festive mood.

The comic characters in the Berkeley production were not so strongly individualised; essentially, they stood for attitudes for or against revelry. The household seemed a united group. Feste was set a little apart by his professionalism, but was essentially part of the same world. Many of the jokes had to do with music. Sir Andrew made his first entrance through the musicians' gallery while Maria and Sir Toby were arguing about him. He got hold of the bass viol just in time to inspire Toby's praise of his musical talents – which he then proceeded to disprove through the excruciating noises he made. The musicians wrested the instrument from him, and he escaped from the ensuing quarrel as a perfect illustration of Maria's analysis of his self-defeating combination of quarrelsomeness and cowardice. Only Malvolio was uninvolved with the musical side of the production, although it is probable that in his courtship of Olivia he is meant to sing a snatch of a popular song, 'Please one and please all'. His stiffness seemed the more unnatural because he was comparatively young, but the production played down his humiliation, which seemed unlikely to have any lasting effects on his resilient ego. In the 'dark house' scene the emphasis was on Feste's virtuosity, and the difficult double-talk was made easier by the fact that the 'real' Sir Topas, the priest who had already appeared in earlier scenes, walked with a stick: thus, Feste was able to accompany his trick voice with a crescendo and diminuendo on the stick which mimicked the priest's arrival and departure.

Interestingly, the four productions differed from each other far more in their attitudes to Olivia's household than in their treatment of the joke played on Malvolio, which they saw as something that began by being funny but went on too long. This is probably the modern consensus on the subject, although I have read of a Malvolio who was presented, the reviewer thought, like Christ in *Ecce Homo* pictures; he remained onstage to the end, 'crouching half-naked in a corner in utter shame and humiliation' (Klaus Bartenschlager, *Shakes-*

*peare Quarterly 71*, 1981, p. 387). It also appears to be taken for granted that there is pathos in the comic characters as well as the romantic ones. Even at Berkeley there was no attempt to conceal the harshness of Toby's last words to Sir Andrew, though they were quickly cut by the entrance of Sebastian. And, after Malvolio's exit, Olivia looked uneasily after him and, intending to be sympathetic, began 'He hath been . . .'. But she could not resist using the word 'notorious', one of his pet expressions. Her lips twitched, the characters caught one anothers' eyes, and they all burst into relieved laughter.

All four of the productions which I have been discussing were much enjoyed by their audiences, and I chose to write about them because I enjoyed them myself. The fact that some of the interpretations contradicted each other made no difference to the effect of any single performance. At the theatre, one lives in the present; what matter is what is happening at the time, not whether something better could have been happening instead. The desire to find a definitive performance corresponds to the desire for an absolute standard in literary criticism. I am prepared to accept the hypothetical existence of such absolutes, but their existence in practice is constantly called into question by the experience of theatre-going. I do not share the frequent academic distrust of directors. They run much greater risks in producing a play than I do in writing about it: they have to pay attention to all its lines, not just the ones that favour their hypothesis, and their audience will react instantly, sometimes cruelly, if it thinks they have got something wrong.

# READING LIST

TEXTS

*Twelfth Night, A New Variorum*, ed. H. H. Furness (Philadelphia and London, 1901). Despite its date, this is still worth seeking out in a library. The appendix includes a number of interesting extracts from reviews of the play in production.

*Twelfth Night*, ed. J. M. Lothian and T. W. Craik (New Arden Shakespeare, 1975). The introduction and notes contain much interesting material about the staging of the play.

*Twelfth Night*, ed. M. M. Mahood (New Penguin Shakespeare, 1968). Pleasantly written introduction; the best inexpensive edition.

*Twelfth Night*, the BBC TV Shakespeare edition, 1979. Contains comments by director and actors in the television production (with photographs).

BACKGROUND

Extracts from some of the play's possible sources can be found in the Arden and Variorum editions and in Geoffrey Bullough, *Narrative and Dramatic Sources of Shakespeare*, vol. 2 (Routledge & Kegan Paul, London; Columbia UP, New York, 1958). *Gl'Ingannati*, tr. Bruce Penman, is available in a full, unexpurgated version in *Five Italian Renaissance Comedies*, ed. Bruce Penman (Penguin, London, 1968). Barnaby Riche's story of Apolonius and Silla is reprinted in *Elizabethan Love Stories*, ed. T. B. J. Spencer (Penguin, London 1968). L. G. Salingar, 'The Design of *Twelfth Night*', *Shakespeare Quarterly 9* (1958) pp. 117–39, is a very full study of the play in relation to its sources and the festive background. C. L. Barber, *Shakespeare's Festive Comedy* (Princeton UP, 1959) sets the early comedies and histories in the context of holiday customs and attitudes. Enid Welsford, *The Fool* (Faber and Faber, London, 1935) gives the historical context of Feste, while M. C. Bradbrook has a chapter on 'The New Clown: Robert Armin', his literary works and his possible influence on Shakespeare, in her *Shakespeare the Craftsman* (Chatto & Windus, London, 1969).

CRITICISM

A useful collection, which includes extracts from early accounts of the play and the Barber and Bradbrook chapters mentioned above, is *Twelfth Night: A Casebook*, ed. D. J. Palmer (Macmillan, London, 1972).

Anne Barton, '*As You Like It* and *Twelfth Night*: Shakespeare's Sense of an Ending', *Shakespearian Comedy*, Stratford upon Avon Studies 14 (Edward Arnold, London, 1972).

Ralph Berry, 'The Season of *Twelfth Night*', in *Changing Styles in Shakespeare* (Allen & Unwin, London, 1981), and '*Twelfth Night*: the Experience of the Audience', *Shakespeare Survey 34* (1981), pp. 111–120.

J. R. Brown, 'Directions for *Twelfth Night*', from *Shakespeare's Plays in Performance* (Edward Arnold, London, 1966; Penguin, London, 1979; also reprinted in *Casebook*); *Shakespeare's Dramatic Style* (Heinemann, London, 1970), includes close study of several extracts from *Twelfth Night*.

Bertrand Evans, *Shakespeare's Comedies* (Clarendon Press, Oxford, 1960), emphasises the element of intrigue and deception.

Harley Granville-Barker, 'Director's Preface to *Twelfth Night*', from his acting edition (1912), reprinted in the Signet edition of the play, is still a perceptive and provocative discussion.

Harold Jenkins, 'Shakespeare's *Twelfth Night*', Rice Institute Pamphlet XLV (1959), reprinted in K. Muir (ed.), *Shakespeare: The Comedies, a Collection of Critical Essays* (Prentice-Hall, Englewood Cliffs, N.J., 1965).

Emrys Jones, *Scenic Form in Shakespeare* (Clarendon Press, Oxford, 1971), mentions the play only incidentally, but offers a fresh approach to the study of dramatic style.

Clifford Leech, '*Twelfth Night' and Shakespearean Comedy* (Toronto UP, 1965), consists of three lectures; one is a well-balanced account of *Twelfth Night*.

Alexander Leggatt, *Shakespeare's Comedy of Love* (Methuen, London, 1974).

Interesting accounts of specific productions, and of the play's acting tradition, may be found in:

Hugh Hung, *Old Vic Prefaces* (Routledge & Kegan Paul, London, 1966).

Gāmini Salgādo, *Eyewitnesses of Shakespeare* (Sussex UP, 1975), which includes some famous accounts of performers in *Twelfth Night*.

A. C. Sprague, *Shakespeare and the Actors* (Harvard UP, Cambridge, Mass., 1944), which has several pages on eighteenth- and nineteenth-century stage business in the play.

A. C. Sprague and J. C. Trewin, *Shakespeare's Plays Today* (Sidgwick & Jackson, London, 1970).

J. C. Trewin, *Going to Shakespeare* (Allen & Unwin, London, 1978).

Stanley Wells, *Royal Shakespeare* (Manchester UP and Furman Studies, 1976), which contains a very full account of the 1969–71 RSC production.

Audrey Williamson, *Old Vic Drama* (Rockliff, London, 1948) and *Old Vic Drama 2* (Rockliff, London, 1957).

*Shakespeare Survey 32* (1979) was devoted to Shakespeare's middle period comedies and contains several excellent essays on *Twelfth Night* as well as a survey by M. M. Mahood of criticism of the comedies.

# INDEX OF NAMES

FOR READER'S NOTES